MORE PRAISE FOR
LET THE DOGS SPEAK!

"I'm spreading the word about this collection of knowledge like I spread my fur – everywhere I can!"

–*Khyra, Siberian Husky - Khyra's Khorner*
(http://khyraskhorner.blogspot.com/)

"A tail-thumping page-turner!"

–*Kahn, Career Change Guide Dog Puppy*

"A riveting book that brings the reader into the world of a working dog. I give it three paws up!"

–*Patrina, CCI Facility Dog, ECLC of New Jersey*

LET THE DOGS SPEAK!

PUPPIES IN TRAINING TELL THE STORY OF CANINE COMPANIONS FOR INDEPENDENCE®

BY MARIANNE MCKIERNAN

ILLUSTRATED BY PENNY BLANKENSHIP

Booktrope Editions
Seattle WA 2013

*All of Author's royalties donated
to Canine Companions for Independence®*

Illustrations by Penny Blankenship

Cover Images Copyright © 2013 Penny Blankenship

Edited by Jane Radke Slade

Entries from the DogBlogs appear with the permission of KMGH-TV, Denver.

The following individuals have generously granted permission to use edited versions of previously published material for this book: Donna Black Sword, Amy Thompson, Pauline Lewis, M-L and Bill Reinking, Jill Exposito, Kevin O'Grady, Vanessa Graziano, Elizabeth Holman, Carol Cornwall, Stan Sander, Jeremy Miller, Regina Benjamin, Dr. Dean Vicksman, Stuart Wahrenbrock, David Ball, and Cheryl Porter-Avino.

PRINT ISBN 978-1-935961-18-5

EPUB ISBN 978-1-62015-125-9

For further information regarding permissions, please contact info@booktrope.com.

Library of Congress Control Number: 2012956019

F irst and foremost, this book is dedicated to John, my beloved and my friend, who famously suggested, "Maybe we should look into raising a service dog puppy," and has yet to say, "Maybe it's time we took a break." One of the many reasons I love him.

This book is also dedicated to Trevin I, Stryker I, Rolly II, Hudson IV, Parker II, Ross VI, Mars I, Rocket I, and Jeb II. Heart dogs, all.

TABLE OF CONTENTS

INTRODUCTION

I n 2001 my husband, John, and I decided that a service dog puppy in training would be the perfect addition to our household, which already included Madeleine the Greyhound, Midden the Airedale-Chow mix, and kitties Drizzle and D'Artagnan. Because Canine Companions for Independence was the oldest service dog organization in the U.S., with an excellent reputation, and because it had a local office in Colorado Springs, we decided it was the best fit for us. After mailing a written application, completing a phone interview with the puppy program manager, and surviving a home visit with a current puppy raiser ("Please make us look good!" I begged our pets), we were approved as Canine Companions volunteer puppy raisers. Our first puppy, Trevin, arrived at Denver International Airport on October 17, 2001, and life has never been the same.

We were looking for a fun, shared activity and a chance to do something nice for someone else. What we found was so much bigger. It's as though we were scavenging for lost change on the beach and discovered Blackbeard's treasure chest *and* the lost city of Atlantis. With sprinkles.

The community we found within Canine Companions is more than a group of people sharing a common interest, or even a common goal; it's a family.

We expected to enjoy the puppy we raised, but we never expected how much fun we'd have with the other puppy raisers, or how central to our lives they would become. We have dogs-in-law: people in every region that we are connected to because we've raised littermates. We have the "Denver Village," our close puppy raiser friends and graduates, people with whom we go to class, socialize, trade puppies, and share experiences. I can no longer imagine life without a leash in my hand.

The DogBlog started as a lark. I began working at KMGH-TV 7News, the ABC affiliate in Denver, in the spring of 2002. My Canine

Companions pups were a welcome addition to the station, often providing comic relief, and sometimes comfort, to stressed co-workers. "I need a minute with the puppy," is an oft-heard phrase when someone is having a difficult day or working on a troubling story.

In the spring of 2007 we were looking for ways to attract viewers to our website. I offered to write a blog about the Canine Companions pups, calling it simply "The DogBlog" at first, writing twelve blog entries before Hudson, our fourth puppy, went off to professional training. Because I was having fun, I kept going when we got our fifth puppy, renaming it Parker's DogBlog. Over 270 entries and five dogs later, the DogBlog is still going strong. Despite the reach of the Internet, I'm still stunned when a seemingly random person in a far-away state comments on the DogBlog, or when I meet a fan in public. The DogBlog has fans! Who knew?

This book is a collection of posts from the DogBlog, edited so that they tell the story of Canine Companions for Independence, and the stories of many amazing puppies in training, in one mirthful, tearful, joyful reading. I'm delighted for this opportunity to introduce new readers to the amazing world of Canine Companions. Say, we always need puppy raisers—how about YOU?

HUDSON

SAYING GOODBYE
TO SAY HELLO

Hudson, the fourth puppy we raised for Canine Companions, arrived via flight angel in Denver with his sister Haji on January 7, 2006. Hudson arrived about six weeks before our third puppy, Rolly, turned in, so we took Rolly along to meet his new "brother." Haji's puppy raisers and several other Denver puppy raisers showed up to welcome the new pups. As you might imagine, two adorable puppies and an entourage attracted the attention of other travelers, so it turned into quite a welcoming party. There's nothing cuter than a tiny puppy in a cape.

Hudson was half Labrador Retriever, half Golden Retriever, but he looked like a black Lab. He was a tall, leggy boy with a big, square head who loved to be told he was gorgeous. Hudson would actually pause to look at his reflection in store windows and mirrors—he *knew* he was gorgeous! He flirted outrageously with teenage girls and young women. We took him to a calendar signing for the Hooter Girls, and the photo tells it all: six beautiful girls, with Hudson in the middle, grinning.

He had a sense of humor and made us laugh; for instance, he used his bone as a skateboard to propel himself around the kitchen. He had the "Baumann wiggle," which means he wagged his whole back end when happy. The funniest thing about Hudson was his fear of butter. One day I took a stick of butter from the refrigerator and started to unwrap it. Hudson had a complete meltdown, racing from the room in terror. "Look, Hudson," I pleaded. "It's just butter."   No dice. He'd just spent a few days with another puppy raiser, so I called Elizabeth and said: "Now, you can be honest with me, and I promise I won't be mad... Did you butter my dog?" After she stopped laughing she assured me that no buttering of dogs had occurred. He always reacted the same way when shown a stick of butter; I even asked the trainers about it, and they assured me that no dog had ever been released for butter phobia.

Hudson was our Zen dog, calm and grounded, wise and noble. We had his aura photographed (as one does) on vacation in Sedona, and the readers all said they had never seen such a deep blue and purple aura, indicating that he was meant to be a healer.

This book begins where the DogBlog did, just as Hudson's time with us was winding down.

HUDSON'S DOGBLOG

WORKING LIKE A DOG

Hudson here. I am the Canine Correspondent for 7News, which is where Marianne works as a producer for the Call 7 investigative and consumer advocacy unit.

All well and good, but what do *I* do at 7News? Here's a typical day for me:

9:00-9:30	Attend the morning news meeting; accept pats and adoration from producers, reporters, and photographers and hope someone pitches a dog story for the newscast;
9:30-10:45	Nap in Marianne's office;
10:45-Noon	Greet guests for the 11 a.m. broadcast (I am especially fond of the staff members from various animal shelters and the pets they bring with them);
12:15	Take a short walk outside;
12:30-1:30	Sit in the doorway of Marianne's office and monitor employees as they return from lunch

	(sadly, they never bring me doggie bags, but I continue to hold out hope);
1:45	Get a big, slurpy drink from my dish and then lay my dripping muzzle in someone's lap;
1:48-4:00	Nap under Marianne's desk;
4:00 until we leave	Yawn, stretch, and stare pointedly at the clock until Marianne realizes it's time to go home for DINNER, my favorite time of day (after breakfast).

Chow for now!
Hudson

DOGGEREL

Marianne and I ran errands on Saturday. Afterwards, I was dozing in the back seat and she was listening to the radio when I heard Garrison Keillor reading poetry on *A Prairie Home Companion*. Here's something I'll bet you didn't know: Dogs are excellent poets.

Humans think we're dreaming about rabbits, squeaky toys, and squirrels, and sure, some of the time we are, but more often than not we're working on a tricky quatrain or trying to think of a word that rhymes with "leash."

Different breeds specialize in different forms. Border Collies create free verse with no punctuation (they love e.e. cummings), Bull Terriers enjoy nonsense rhymes, Akitas write haiku, Borzois compose sonnets, and French Bulldogs specialize in terse verse. Poodles, for all their airs and graces, love limericks, particularly the naughty ones. ("There once was a bitch from Nantucket...")

We like to talk about our poems, too. I met a French Bulldog on Saturday at PetSmart who recited a terse verse she'd composed that afternoon:

> *Grinning wife, holding adorable puppy, explaining*
> *to exasperated husband why she brought home yet*
> *another dog:*
>
> *Pug mug.*

We had a good laugh over that one!

Here's a poem I composed recently during my post-dinner nap:

> **The Green Towel**
> by Hudson
>
> *Rain*
> *Dank, earthy smells*
> *Soggy grass*
> *Glorious mud*
> *Joyous gallop*
> *Exquisitely wet feet*
> *But then ...*
> *"Hudson, here!"*
> *She takes the dry green towel*
> *And wipes all traces of Spring*
> *From my feet.*
> *I look longingly out the door*
> *Past the muddy green towel*
> *That now smells like my paws.*

Chow for now!
Hudson

Puppy Classes

Someone at work recently asked if I was homeschooled to learn all my commands. Nope, I go to class with my Canine Companions pals two or three times each month, with lots of homework in between. We have a special trainer named Amy who instructs the puppy raisers on how to teach us the commands, and then we practice over and over and over until the next class. Good thing I work for treats. Otherwise, it could get pretty tedious.

Amy makes classes fun. For example, at one class she asked us to lie down in two lines facing each other. We took turns waiting at the top of the line until our puppy raiser called "Here!" from the end of the line. The tricky part was walking or running straight to our puppy raiser without stopping to sniff another puppy or say hello. We all did it perfectly, much to the amazement of the humans. Oh ye of little faith!

Another time, Amy set up stations around the room for practicing our commands. I liked doing sequences of *sit-down-sit-down-sit-down* (the puppy raisers call those "puppy push-ups") in front of a blowing fan, but some dogs complained because they didn't like getting their hair mussed. *eyeroll* Girls!

At another station I maintained a *sit-stay* while Marianne ran a vacuum around me. It was a little uncomfortable, but I took deep breaths and reminded myself that the vacuum is not a monster looking to eat my tail.

At the last station, I practiced *down-stay* on a dog bed. "Jeez Hudson, that's not so hard," you say. I say "HA!" The bed was full of wonderful doggy smells, but I wasn't allowed to sniff it; apparently, sniffing is not considered good service dog behavior. Then, just to make it even harder, Marianne dropped carrots on the floor! We're not allowed to eat any food off the floor, no matter how yummy it is. I love carrots, so this was really difficult. She even dropped one ON MY PAW (Oh, the temptation!), but I left it alone. She told me I was a Very Good Boy and gave me a carrot as a reward.

One game, Tic Tac Toe, was almost ridiculously complex, but I love a challenge. Amy made a grid out of tape on the floor and divided us into two teams. The puppy raisers took turns putting each of us into a *sit-stay* or *down-stay* on a square. Apparently there was some strategy involved, because the puppy raisers were very picky about exactly which square was chosen each time. I just wanted the one that smelled the best.

To make it even more challenging, we weren't allowed to move even a toe out of the square, sniff the floor, or say "Hello!" to the puppy in the next square. I lost because my tail went over the line out of the square. Stupid tail has a mind of its own. It knocks stuff off the coffee table all the time.

Chow for now!
Hudson

GUEST BLOGGER: CANINE ADVICE COLUMNIST "DEAR LABBY" EXPLAINS SERVICE DOG ETIQUETTE

Dear Labby,

I love to eat everything off the ground: dropped food, piles of dust, sticks, rocks, bottle caps—just about anything I can find! My puppy raisers tell me I shouldn't do this, but how can I resist when there are so many temptations? And why is their pet dog allowed to eat things I'm not?

Also, Marianne won't let me sniff anything when we're out and about. What is it with humans, anyway? Don't they know how to communicate?

Finally, I get reprimanded when I bark; Marianne says, "It's not your job." Why not? Isn't barking a part of being a dog? And why are the keeper dogs allowed to bark? I have things to say too!

Confused,
Hudson

Dear Hudson,

It's true: service dog rules are different than pet dog rules. It is not OK to eat things off the floor because you have a public image to maintain, and you're supposed to be working, not snacking. Pet dogs (or, as you say, "keeper dogs") may have fewer rules, but they don't get to go to movies or grocery stores like you do. And remember, you may think that a bottle cap is a tasty treat, but you'll be sorry when the vet decides he has to surgically remove it. Trust me on this.

As for sniffing, remember that when you're working you're supposed to be discreet. So a quick sniff is OK, but leave the investigative and hobby sniffing for your off-duty hours. And no licking either! Canine Companions pups have a standard to uphold. (Kissing your puppy raiser at home is allowed.)

Now barking … Well, barking is complicated. Some dogs bark to alert their families to danger ("Intruder! Mailman! Scary squirrel!"). Other dogs bark to talk to their friends in the neighborhood ("Hi, I'm Fang and I'm playing with a ball!"). Some small, nervous dogs bark just because they can ("I'm three pounds of fluff and no brain but I have a shrill voice!"). Sorry, that was doggist of me. Ahem.

Hudson, old buddy, your job is to learn to help someone with a disability. Nonstop BARKBARKBARKBARKBARK for an assistance dog means "My partner needs help right now!" *Speak* is a very important Canine Companions command, so barking should not be used for frivolous stuff like "Gimme another cookie!" or "UPS truck going by!" or "Yikes, snake on the deck!" Leave that nonsense to the silly keeper dogs.

Love,
Labby

FIELD TRIPS

Did you think that field trips were just for little kids? Not at all! Sometimes we go on field trips for puppy class. Amy tries to pick places that will help us experience new things in a controlled environment. A good example is the annual trip to a fire station.

I bet you're wondering what that trip has to do with being a service dog. Well, it's possible that our partner might have a medical emergency (or, Dog forbid, a fire) and it's helpful if we are already acquainted with emergency people and equipment. Part of it is just getting used to noises like sirens, alarms, and even the loud motor and exhaust on the fire engine. But the scariest part is when a fireman comes out in full gear, including the oxygen tank that makes him sound like Darth Vader. "Hudson, I am your father." (Sorry, bad joke.) Anyhow, the fireman kneels down to eye level and lets us approach. He pets us and gives us cookies. Pretty soon we're all relaxed and don't care that he looks weird or sounds scary. There's a risk with this class: sometimes the firemen have to leave for an actual emergency! Then we hear the sirens and see them in gear for real. It's very exciting, I have to say. After class is over we pose for pictures on the fire engine.

My favorite field trip was a scavenger hunt race at PETCO. Amy gave the puppy raisers a list of items to collect in a shopping buggy while keeping us pups under control AND giving us specific commands. Marianne and I ran really fast around the store, I did all the commands just right, and we won the race!　Marianne gave me a big hug and told me how clever I was.

Our strangest class was at a bowling alley. We weren't allowed to explore the lanes or sniff the funny-looking shoes the puppy raisers all put on. Never having been to a bowling alley before, I was stunned when the puppy raisers started heaving big, heavy balls down the lanes at some tall white stickish things. Sometimes all the sticks fell down, but not very often, so the puppy raisers would heave the balls at them again. We all wanted to chase the balls down the lane and push the sticks over, but the puppy raisers wouldn't let us. "*Assistance dogs*," we said. "We can help you with this! It's right up our alley!" *snicker* But the puppy raisers made us lie down and stay still. I bet Marianne's score would have been a lot higher if she'd let me help. HA.

Chow for now!
Hudson

WONDER DOGS

Happy holidays, DogBlog readers! I have to tell you, I was absolutely nonplussed when a fat man with a white beard dressed in a red suit came into the Canine Companions holiday party giving a loud *ho-ho-ho* command, over and over. The command must have been for the humans in the room, because we didn't respond at all and received no corrections. None of us knew what to make of it. We posed for photos with the fat man, and my nose told me right away that it was my Uncle Kevin, who is raising Phlox. None of the dogs were fooled, though the people seemed to be. Human noses are a disgrace.

Anyhow, later in the week we drove to Sedona for a holiday vacation. It was a beautiful place of red rocks and snow. We did lots of hikes and then lounged around the fireplace in our condo, where Marianne read, John worked crossword puzzles, and I napped. All that hiking wore me out; I am still a growing puppy, after all.

One day Marianne suggested wandering through art galleries and shops instead of a hike. I got a ton of attention every place we went, which slowed things down quite a lot, but Marianne and John didn't seem to care. In one art gallery I got a whiff of dog. Sure enough, we rounded a corner into another room and there was a yellow Lab service dog! I could tell because she was wearing a red cape (not Canine Companions blue) and she was sitting next to a woman in a wheelchair.

The dog saw us and nodded at me. The woman turned around to see what the dog was looking at and laughed. "Bella always sees other service dogs before I do," she said. "She ignores regular dogs, but not service dogs."

We walked over, and Marianne and John introduced themselves and me to Fran and Bella. Bella wagged her tail politely, and I tried to get closer for a sniff. Marianne sharply corrected me and made me sit. "He's still learning," she apologized. I was mortified.

Fran asked, "May I pet him?"

Marianne said "Absolutely!" and Fran reached over and patted my head.

"Hudson is gorgeous! I'm sure he's going to make a great partner for someone." I sat a little taller.

"We hope so," said John. "How long have you and Bella been together?"

"Just over three years, and I can't imagine how I coped before," Fran said. "I have a hard time reaching lights, and she turns them on for me. I drop stuff a lot, and she picks up anything and everything." Bella wagged her tail. "Would you like a demonstration?" We all nodded. Fran took off her glasses and dropped them on the floor. Bella immediately walked over, gently picked them up, and stood at Fran's side as Fran took the glasses and put them back on. Next, Fran took a dime from the wallet that she had in her lap and dropped it on the floor.

"WOW!" John said as Bella carefully picked up the dime and dropped it in Fran's hand. "That's incredible!"

Fran stroked Bella's head. "Yes, she is my Wonder Dog. My life has changed in so many ways since I got her. Before, I was afraid to travel by myself, but now we take trips together at least once a month. I can visit family and friends, rather than always having to ask them to visit me. I love live music and theater, so we go to a lot of concerts and plays. If a friend wants to come along that's fine, but I have the confidence to go on my own now that Bella is with me. I can go to doctors' appointments and run errands without having to ask for help. I have my life back!"

Marianne looked a little watery-eyed. "Hudson, are you listening to this?"

I wagged my tail. Of course I was.

Fran gave me one last pat. "I have a feeling Hudson is going to be some lucky person's very own Wonder Dog. Have a good visit in Sedona!" She and Bella rolled-strolled away.

The next store we went into smelled funny ("Incense," Marianne told me) and was crammed full of tinkly bells, rocks, candles, fairy statues, fountains, crystals, and books.

"Ooh!" Marianne exclaimed. "They can take photos of our auras!"

John got a devilish gleam in his eye. "Let's get Hudson's aura photographed."

The photographer looked at me dubiously. "I've never done a dog before." He shrugged. "OK, let's try it." He placed my front paws on two metal human foot-shaped plates. "Hold still," he told me and looked through the lens of a large camera. A few seconds later he said he was done and it would take a few minutes for the photo to develop. Marianne wandered over to the books. John went to the counter to pay for my photo. I lay down for a nap.

"Oh, my!" said the cashier. "Look at this photo!" She held up a photo of me surrounded by a purplish-blue halo of light, and the other workers in the store gathered around.

"Wow, that's amazing!" said one.

"I've never seen an aura that color before," said another. They all turned and stared at me.

"What's it mean?" asked John.

"That's a good color, right?" said Marianne anxiously.

The photographer nodded. "Oh yeah, it's an awesome color. That's the color for a healer. He's going to do some fantastic work in his life as a healer."

I already knew this of course, but it made me feel good to hear someone else say it.

"Good Wonder Dog," Marianne said, giving me a hug.

Chow for now!
Hudson

HUDSON SAYS GOODBYE & GUEST BLOGGER "DEAR LABBY" OFFERS WORDS OF WISDOM ABOUT PROFESSIONAL TRAINING

"I'm leaving on a jet plane; don't know if I'll be back again ..."

Bet you didn't know I could sing, did you? I'm off to professional training with seven of my Denver classmates. We're pretty excited about it, but our puppy raisers seem rather glum. I don't understand why. Marianne says she'll explain later. In the meantime, my classmates and I have questions about professional training.

Dear Labby,

I'm going to professional training (which my puppy raiser calls "Canine Companions College") in Oceanside, California. I'm nervous! What will it be like? Who will be my trainer? I'm afraid I won't get hugged and petted like I do now. Help!

Signed,
Phlox

Dear Phloxie,

You're going to LOVE professional training, I promise! You'll make lots of new friends, and your sister Perrin will be there too. Maybe you'll get to be roommates! Your dorm room will be very nice, with heated floors, a skylight, and music. I don't know who your trainer will be, but rest assured that he or she will love you every bit as much as your puppy raisers do. You'll still get cuddle time every day, frequent play time in the yard with your classmates, and lots of attention from the rest of the staff. Hugs are as much a part of your training day as lessons. Have fun!

Love,
Labby

*   *   *

Dear Labby,

I'm a laid-back kind of dog. Some days I want to work, and others I want to sleep in. Will the professional training course be too much for me? Will the trainer let me sleep in sometimes? I'm afraid the commands will be too hard.

In fear,
Hudson

Dear Hudson,

Never fear, you'll get plenty of rest at professional training. Each trainer has six or seven other dogs on his or her "string." While the trainer is working with one dog, the rest can nap in crates in the training room. You may find you're more interested in watching your classmates than napping because you're going to be learning cool stuff like how to open doors, turn on lights, and retrieve all kinds of things. And no, professional training will not be too hard for you, silly boy.

Love,
Labby

*   *   *

Dear Labby,

How long is professional training? What if I don't like it or decide that I don't want to be a working dog? Was Thomas Wolfe wrong—can I go home again?

Signed,
Perrin

Dear Perrin,

I think you really ought to give it the old college try, at least for the first semester. Professional training is usually two or three semesters (six to nine months). You may find that you really like working and can't wait to be matched to your forever partner. In any case, one of the best things about Canine Companions is that they understand that some dogs don't want to work—they want to be adored pets. And that's OK, because it means that the dogs who graduate really love their jobs.

So, it's all up to you. If you decide you want to be a Canine Companions graduate dog, then pay attention in class, mind your trainer, and do your best. If you decide it's not right for you, let your trainer know and you'll be released from the program and become a "change of career" dog. Either way, you'll be someone's best friend! And yes, if you decide being an assistance dog is not for you, either your puppy raisers will welcome you home, or the universe will direct you to the perfect someone who has been searching for a puppy just like you.

Love,
Labby

*   *   *

Dear Labby,

I'm very excited about professional training and I think I will do well. I'm not sure what my job will be. What if I pick the wrong one and want to change my mind? Can you help me decide?

Signed,
Maddy

Dear Maddy,

You don't need to worry about this! Your trainer will work with you and help you decide what your job will be. You might be a Service Dog, opening doors, turning on lights, retrieving dropped items, and perhaps even pulling a wheelchair. Or you might become a Skilled Companion, helping with physical tasks and emotional bonding. Your trainer might decide you'd be best as a Facility Dog, assisting someone like a teacher or therapist at work. You might even be suited as a Hearing Dog, letting your partner know when the phone rings, the baby cries, or some other noise beckons your partner's attention.

Your trainer will help you pick the best job for your skills. Good luck and send me an invitation to your graduation, OK?

Love,
Labby

* * *

Dear Labby,

I've been told I might be picked for the breeding program. What the heck does that mean? I was all set to learn cool stuff at professional training, like how to fetch sodas from the refrigerator and help with the laundry.

Signed,
Haji

Dear Haji,

Wow—what an honor! Canine Companions has its own breeding program, and only the best of the best, the cream of the crop, are selected as breeders. In that case you'll go live with a breeder caretaker near Santa Rosa, California. Breeder girls usually have four or five litters of puppies in their careers. When the puppies are eight weeks old, the breeder caretaker takes them to the Canine Companions National Headquarters in Santa Rosa. They are vaccinated, tattooed, bathed, and then sent to puppy raisers all over the country. A service dog helps one person in a career, but just think how many people you might help through your wonderful children! Send me lots of pictures, and make sure at least one of your pups comes to Denver so I can play with it.

Love,
Labby

GUEST BLOGGER MARIANNE EXPLAINS TURN-IN

Bittersweet (adj.) 1. Bitter and sweet at the same time: bittersweet chocolate. 2. Producing or expressing a mixture of pain and pleasure: a movie with a bittersweet ending. 3. The feeling a puppy raiser has when giving the dog back to Canine Companions at turn-in.

Turn-in: *Returning a puppy to Canine Companions for professional training.*

Hudson is my fourth Canine Companions puppy. By far, the question puppy raisers hear most often is "But don't you get attached? Don't you love them?" Yes, of course we do; we adore these dogs. We couldn't do this if we didn't love the dogs. "But how can you give him up?" is the next question. The glib answer is "With a big box of tissues beforehand, and really big margaritas afterward!"

The real answer is that we're not giving him up; we're giving him back, because he is Canine Companions' dog. Returning him after eighteen months is precisely what John and I signed on for.

Canine Companions trusted us with a priceless eight-week-old bundle of fur, and asked us to take him to class twice a month and teach him thirty commands, feed him premium dog food, groom him weekly (nails, teeth, ears, and coat), provide for his vaccinations and health care, send in monthly status reports, socialize him in all kinds of public settings, play with him, and, oh yeah, give him back after eighteen months or so.

But the biggest, best, and easiest thing that Canine Companions trusted us to do with its puppy was to love him.

And here's the thing: it's really not about us anyhow. It's about someone in need who has completed the application process and is patiently waiting to receive an assistance dog, possibly Hudson. Our hope against hope is that in six to nine months we'll go back to the Canine Companions campus to meet that person and formally hand over Hudson's leash one last time at the graduation ceremony.

Besides being the day that puppies are turned in for professional training, it's also the day that individuals with disabilities, who have attended Canine Companions' intense two-week Team Training, graduate with their new canine partners as "graduate teams." The puppy raisers for those dogs are invited to the ceremony to hand over the leashes—a very moving moment indeed.

So, Friday we will start the next phase of Hudson's life by taking him to Oceanside, California. We'll have a wonderful time that night with our fellow puppy raisers who are also turning in their pups. We'll go out for dinner together and then go back to the hotel and hang out and tell stories about our wonderful dogs, and laugh often. And even though Canine Companions dogs are not allowed to sleep on the puppy raisers' beds, that last night is often the exception to the rule (but you didn't hear it from me).

Saturday morning we'll glumly eat breakfast together and then drive over to the lovely Mission San Luis Rey where the turn-in and graduation ceremony is held. We'll take lots of pictures outside in the gardens of the pups in their special blue matriculation capes, and we'll partake of retail therapy at the Canine Companions gift shop.

The program begins around noon. There are speeches by the staff, a slide show featuring photographs sent by puppy raisers of their little ones in full puppy action, and introductions of puppy raisers and pups as we march across the stage to "Pomp and Circumstance." There are video interviews with each new graduate team, and then proud puppy raisers walk on stage to hand over the leash of the puppy they raised. Sometimes a trainer tells stories about that particular graduating class, and often someone is chosen as class speaker. The ceremony is funny, poignant, heartwarming, and there's not a dry eye in the house when it's over. There's a very good reason that full-sized boxes of tissues are scattered around the auditorium.

And then it's time.

As much as we'd like to linger at the Mission, we'll drag ourselves over to the Canine Companions campus where the actual turn-in takes place. John and I will give Hudson big hugs and tell him how much we love him and how proud we are of him. We'll take off his pretty Celtic collar and leather leash, and put on a plain blue Canine Companions collar and leash. One last hug, and then we will hand Hudson's leash to a kind volunteer who will lead him off to meet his roommate and get settled into his new home.

Like all of the dogs, I expect Hudson to trot off with nary a backward glance at us, a bounce in his step, eager to go play with the other dogs. At that moment John and I will have Hudson-shaped holes in our hearts the size of Texas. It is both the end and the beginning, bittersweet.

We'll join the other teary, sniffling puppy raisers to drink margaritas and talk about the graduation ceremony. Watching twelve people receive the Canine Companions dogs they've been dreaming about, sometimes for years, is a powerful reminder of why we do this. Hearing a recipient say, "I will be able to do things for myself now; this dog will give me back my life," or a parent say, "My child spoke for the first time in two years because he wanted to call his dog," makes handing over the leash a lot easier. We will voice the hope that maybe in six months' time they will be talking about our dogs.

I'll always have a Hudson-shaped space in my heart, just like I have Trevin-, Stryker-, and Rolly-shaped spaces. But it helps to know that Hudson has happily begun the next step toward his destiny, and we'll eagerly wait for his monthly report cards, hoping for the best.

In the meantime, we have a nine-week-old bundle of fur named Parker waiting for us at home.

PARKER

The Community
Expands

I decided to fly to San Diego to pick up Parker rather than having him shipped via cargo. A kind puppy raiser picked up Parker from the Canine Companions office in Oceanside and met me at the airport, saving me the hassle of renting a car and driving to Oceanside and back. Timing was tight, so Parker had a quick *hurry* (our command for toileting) before we dashed to security. Once we made it through, I stuffed Parker into the soft-sided travel crate and ran to the gate. Parker was so exhausted that he did not make a peep for the next three hours. My seatmate didn't even know there was a puppy under the seat until I picked up the crate when we landed. Parker didn't wake up until I lifted him out of the crate for a drink and a little walk before we got in the car and headed home. He made up for it when we got home, chasing Hudson around the backyard at full tilt.

Parker was three-fourths Lab, one-fourth Golden Retriever, and he looked like a yellow Lab. As a young puppy, Parker was mischievous and had a little bit of attitude. He was inquisitive, the only pup we've had that was fascinated by noises. He would sit in front of the dishwasher when it was running, cocking his head to catch the changes in sound as it cycled. He was attracted to goats and miniature horses and would have liked one of his own, please. As he grew older he lost the attitude and became sweet and cuddly.

Parker was a confident pup, willing to work, especially if there was a camera involved. One drawback of bringing Parker to work at the TV station was that Parker quickly considered himself "talent" and perked up whenever he saw a camera, still or video, posing, unasked, for best effect. One day we were using him to "narrate" a story about a local pet therapy program. Alan, the photographer, asked me to have Parker walk from Point A to Point B in the newsroom while Mike, the anchor, was broadcasting live. I thought Alan was out of his mind, given the number of distractions and things that could easily go wrong. (Among other horrifying possibilities, I envisioned Parker trying to climb into Mike's lap.) I gulped, put Parker on his mark at Point A, told him to *stay*, walked to Point B and held my breath. "Action!" On cue, Parker casually strolled to me and sat, looking neither to the right nor the left, hitting his mark perfectly. Alan joked, "I wish some of the reporters followed directions that well."

If Canine Companions professional training didn't work out, we figured Parker could have a successful future in commercial work.

PARKER'S DOGBLOG

THE TALENT HAS LANDED

Well! Hudson told me I'd like it here at 7News but I had no idea just how dog-friendly (or is it dog-crazy?) people here are. Man, I can hardly get my morning and afternoon naps in between visitors and requests for me to attend meetings. You know, I don't kiss and tell, but if I had a Milk Bone for every smooch, I'd be one fat puppy.

So, a little background. I am one of eleven pups in my litter. All the pups in a litter have names with the same first letter, so we're a P litter. My siblings are Patrina, Penela, Piute, Pixel, Peggy, Paisley, Pasha, Pippi, Pilot, and Palmer. My mom, Carie, is half Labrador, half Golden Retriever. Her breeder caretaker was also her puppy raiser, so she was raised near Canine Companions headquarters in Santa Rosa, California. Strangely, she wasn't very sad to see us leave. I guess eleven puppies is a lot of work.

My dad is Neese, and he's full Lab. I look a lot like him, I'm told. He was raised by some puppy raisers here in Denver, so I'm sure I'll hear all kinds of cool stories about him. I've heard one rumor about him being kind of a "wild child" as a puppy, but I'm sure that can't be right.

Chow for now!
Parker

PUPPY KINDERGARTEN

Hudson let me try on his extra-large Canine Companions cape before he went off to professional training. I can't wait until I'm big enough to wear that size! Everybody keeps saying I've grown, but I don't feel bigger. Marianne has started to say "Oof!" every time she picks me up. She told me the other day that I'm like bread dough, I keep doubling in size, and then she went to see her chiropractor. Huh. There might be a connection.

I've been to two puppy classes already. Canine Companions pups start with Pre-Puppy Kindergarten, then Puppy Kindergarten (KPT),

then Basic Class, and finally Advanced Class. So far I've learned *sit,
down, shake,* and *speak.* I like *speak* the best, but Marianne doesn't seem
to like it when I show her I know how to do it without being asked.
Jeez, you'd think she would be pleased I learned it so fast. So yeah,
OK, I also know *quiet, no,* and *don't.*

I'm learning *off* too. I hear *off* a lot when I try to climb over a baby
gate or out of my exercise pen ("x-pen"). Hey, I just want to be part of
the action! How am I supposed to pounce on the other dogs or chase
the cats or shred the morning papers if I'm confined in the kitchen?

I'm working on *kennel* (I like that one because it means I get a
cookie and a nap) and *dress,* which is when I have to stand still and let
Marianne put on my cape and Gentle Leader. I am not a big fan of the
Gentle Leader and try to pull it off when she's not looking, but she
catches me every time. The problem with being Puppy #5 is that she's
hip to the tricks.

My least favorite command so far is *wait.* I don't see the point of
wait; I am not a patient puppy. I want <u>what</u> I want <u>when</u> I want it,
which is <u>right now!</u> But I have to *wait* for my food, *wait* to get out of
the crate, *wait* to go out a door, blah blah blah.

SIGH

Chow for now!
Parker

BATHS ARE FOR THE BIRDS

Marianne seems irritated with me. It might have something to do
with what happened yesterday and the recipe I found on her desk
this morning:

Malodorous Mutt Medley

Ingredients:

- One white puppy
- 2 square yards of dirty asphalt
- One dead snake
- One tub of water
- One bottle of shampoo
- Three dog towels
- One Kong toy stuffed with biscuits
- One plastic bag
- One dog crate
- Alcoholic beverage of choice

Directions:

- Walk puppy to car.

- Scold puppy for rolling on asphalt in attempt to remove cape and Gentle Leader.

- Dust off filthy puppy and gingerly place in car. Drive home.

- Take puppy into backyard to brush him. Wonder why puppy is rolling in grass.

- Race across yard. Lift puppy off dead snake. Groan.

- Hold breath, tote puppy at arm's length into house.

- Deposit puppy in bathtub; fill with warm water.

- Apply shampoo with abandon.

- Catch slippery, airborne puppy and wrestle him back into tub.

- Take shampoo bottle away from puppy.

- Scrub thoroughly.

- Dissuade puppy from eating soapsuds and drinking soapy water.

- Drain tub and refill. Rinse puppy.

- Discourage puppy from joyously digging in bathwater.

- Remove dripping, squirming puppy from tub.

- Dry puppy vigorously.

- Remove towel from puppy's mouth and discourage game of tug-of-war.

- Deposit damp puppy in crate with stuffed Kong.

- Dry off walls and floor in bathroom.

- Go to backyard and gingerly pick up dead snake with plastic bag; deposit in outdoor trash container (funeral rites optional).

🐕 Wash hands. Change clothes. Dry hair. Clean water spots off glasses.

🐕 Fix drink. Collapse.

Chow for now!
Parker

SINGING THE PAPERWORK BLUES

I was nibbling on my chewie bone and humming along with a song on the radio this morning. "Nobody knows the trouble I've seen," I warbled.

Marianne looked up from her desk. "Nobody knows the trouble you *are*," she snorted.

Moi? Whatever could she mean?

"Look, Parker," she said. "Kibble doesn't grow on trees. You know I love you, but you have no idea how much money and time I spend on you, do you?"

Well, no. What are a few kibbles after all?

Turns out puppy raisers do a lot more than just fill the food dish every day. Marianne told me they provide all our food, treats, toys, vet care (ugh, shots!), and equipment, like crates, dog beds, exercise pens, collars, and leashes.

In addition, Marianne flew to San Diego to pick me up when I was eight weeks old, and she will take me back to California when it's time for professional training. Marianne jokes that at least I have a full-ride scholarship once I get there.

And yikes, the paperwork she has to do! Puppy raisers have to complete reports every month that detail our weight, what we eat and how much per day, any health issues, the commands we are learning, where and when our puppy classes were held, where we went and what we did each day, and all kinds of behavioral information. Man, there are no secrets at Canine Companions.

Puppy raisers also teach us what NOT to do. This week, for instance, I learned that chewing on my cape is a no-no, chasing the cat is a bad idea, and repeatedly flipping over my water dish earns me a time-out in my crate. HUH. I was ready for a nap anyhow.

I guess this puppy raiser stuff is more complicated than I thought. Marianne says when she returns me to Canine Companions she'll have invested around 12,000 hours and $2,500 in me.

Wow. Good thing she loves me, huh?

Chow for now!
Parker

HERE COMES THE SUN

HOT. Boy, is it HOT. Nobody told me Colorado would be HOT. Yow. I've been able to keep cool at home by relaxing by my wading pool. Ah, life is good.

I have a bone to pick with some of you pet owners. Yeah, you. You know who you are. You're the one who thinks Fido will be lonesome at home, so you take the poor thing with you on your errands.

Trust me, no dog wants to ride around with you when it's hot. Why would we want to be stuck in the car at the grocery store when we could be at home, stretched out on the cool tile floor next to a water dish? Or in the backyard under a nice shady tree with a wading pool handy for quick dips?

Speaking of dips, leaving us in the car is a Very Bad Idea. Yeah, yeah, you say it will be "just a few minutes." But what if you get distracted or delayed?

I had Marianne do some research for me.

I'll bet you didn't know that the temperature in a car rises 19 degrees in 10 minutes, 29 degrees in 20 minutes, and 43 degrees in an hour.

Studies show that cracking the windows doesn't significantly change that, and the temperature rises inside the car even on cool days. If it's seventy two degrees outside, it will be 115 degrees in your car in an hour.

But let's focus on one quick summer errand. There you are in the grocery store, wheeling your cart up and down the aisles, trying to decide what to fix for dinner. It's ninety degrees outside. In the ten minutes you've been in the store, the temperature in your car has risen to 109 degrees. Fido is panting like mad, trying to cool off.

You finish shopping, but checking out takes another ten minutes. The temperature in your car is 119. Fido is dangerously near heat stroke, and may suffer permanent brain damage or even death. DEATH! Do you still think he really wanted to ride to the store with you? Not so much.

Don't get me started on sidewalks and pavement. Hey! You with the shoes! If it's too hot for you to go barefoot, then it's too hot for us, too. Our poor feet get burned, literally burned, by hot pavement.

Let's talk about water. You always carry your fancy-schmancy water bottle for yourself, but do you bring one for Fido? He gets dehydrated too, so make sure you carry lots of water for both of you, whatever activity you're doing together.

And please make sure Fido has lots of fresh water at home. Give him some ice cubes for a treat. The puppy raisers give us "water biscuits" all the time, which we adore. Crunchy, wet, and cold all at the same time—what could be better?

Chow for now!
Parker

WORKING DOGS ROCK!

WOW! I am so jazzed! I met Canine Companions dog Rudy this week. He graduated in August 2006 with Jeremy, who is twenty four and uses a wheelchair.

Rudy goes everywhere with Jeremy, including Rockies games, college, church, the mall, and restaurants. He sleeps on Jeremy's bed (I am SO jealous), and sits next to Jeremy on the couch in the evening when they watch TV (again, JEALOUS!).

I've been watching the reporters at 7News and what they do looks pretty easy. I decided to give it a try and interview Rudy.

PARKER: How did you get matched with Jeremy? What was that experience like?

RUDY: I met Jeremy and his parents in Team Training, which happened after six months of professional training. I was a little nervous, but they seemed so nice that I really wanted to live with them. My new family had a hard time in Team Training--they had to learn everything I know, and how to give my commands with authority. They all worked together on the tests, and we passed!

PARKER: What's it like at Jeremy's house?

RUDY: Jeremy lives with his mom and dad, and they help him do all kinds of fun things with me. We have lots of visits from Jeremy's sisters and their husbands, and Jeremy's aunt and his cousin. They bring their pet dogs over to visit, so we play together when I'm not working with Jeremy.

PARKER: Do you like Colorado?

RUDY: I was raised in southern California, so I had a lot to learn, especially about SNOW! I like it a lot.

PARKER: What's your average day like?

RUDY: Jeremy's dad lets me out before he leaves at 6 a.m., and then rouses Jeremy to feed me breakfast. We may go to college or to the mall and then come home and lie on the sofa together to watch TV. Sometimes Jeremy's parents will take me for a walk in the evening, and I really like that.

PARKER: How do you and Jeremy work together as a team?

RUDY: It took me several months to figure out that Jeremy is a boss, too. His parents finally told me, "Watch Jeremy," and I realized that he was giving me commands. So now I *come* when I'm called, I *sit*, and then I *visit*–put my head on Jeremy's lap for him to pet me. I love that!

PARKER: What's the best part of being a service dog?

RUDY: Jeremy loves showing me off. When we're out in public, people ask him if they can pet me, and he grants permission. Little kids love to pet and hug me. I never get tired of being loved!

PARKER: People are always interested in us. What's the best way for them to ask so that we can get petted? Are there times when Jeremy doesn't want people to pet you?

RUDY: Most people are very respectful and ask "Can I pet your dog?" Sometimes when they don't ask it's a little distracting to me, and I get confused as to whether I'm supposed to respond to them. So I look at Jeremy, and he'll tell me to sit so I can be petted. And then he gives permission.

PARKER: What advice do you have for me?

RUDY: Just work really hard and mind your puppy raisers and your trainer at Canine Companions professional training. Our lives are really interesting when we go out with our people to their jobs, schools, and fun places. Plus, we're loved and needed, and that's the best of all!

Chow for now!
Parker

HUDSON'S FIRST REPORT CARD

As you know, Hudson is in professional training in California. Some of the dogs who went with him have decided that this line of work is not their cup of kibble and have returned home to be keeper dogs (pets). Marianne says they are now Canine Companions "change of career" dogs.

At any rate, Hudson is still in professional training, which is very exciting. We received one short letter from him shortly after turn-in that said he is rooming with Evert and his trainer is Jules. Oh, and he is having fun and enjoying playtime.

Apparently that's not enough information for Marianne, who frets.

"What's the problem? You know he's happy, you know he's having fun, and you know that Jules loves him," I said.

"I know," Marianne admitted, "but I want to know how his classes are going. Is he studying hard, or is he staying up too late? Is he behaving, or is he goofing with the guys, ordering rawhides, drinking too much water, and leading collar raids on the girls' dorm?"

I think I'm too young to understand that last part.

Anyhow, the first report card arrived. My stars and whiskers, the cheering and dancing going on at my house is astonishing, given that it's just because we received a silly email. Pardon me. It's an email with AN ATTACHMENT. Whoopee. Still, Marianne was thrilled.

The first part of the report card had really good news: Hudson passed all of the health and temperament tests! Huzzah.

Jules went on to say, "Hudson plays well with other dogs during community run and seeks me out in the play yard. He is adjusting well to the kennels and has a good energy level for the program."

Sounds like he's kind of a goody four-paws to me, but Marianne was happy about it. In fact, Marianne was delighted to hear that Hudson's only real issue is showing some fear toward "novel stimuli" (she says that's trainer-speak for "new stuff") with a "slow recovery."

"Jeez," I said, "New stuff scares me, too. What's the big deal?"

Marianne explained it to me. Canine Companions trainers aren't overly concerned about a dog reacting to something startling (unless it happens all the time), but they want the dog to shake it off and relax so they can get back to work. It seems that Hudson is a little stressed with professional training life and not settling down after a loud noise (or some other startling event) as fast as Jules would like. However, Jules said that Hudson is already showing improvement.

Best of all, Jules is teaching Hudson some new commands. He's learning to retrieve all kinds of things, and then to hold the item until Jules tells him to give it to her. I'm just working on *fetch*, which is the baby version. I can't wait until I go to professional training and learn the fancy stuff!

Of course, now we have ANOTHER month of fretting until the second report card arrives. I'm not sure I can take the strain. And get this—not only do we fret about Hudson, but Marianne emails the other puppy raisers who have dogs at professional training to find out what their reports say, and they fret COLLECTIVELY.

Humans baffle me; they really do.

Chow for now!
Parker

GUEST BLOGGER "DEAR LABBY": PARKER WANTS FOOD AND JUSTICE

Dear Labby,

Hudson told me to write to you if I have questions. Boy, do I have questions!

First, what is it with the *off* command? The keeper dogs and cats never hear *off*, but I hear it constantly.

And what's the big deal about *sit*? It used to be good enough for Marianne that I sat when she told me to, but now she keeps poking and rearranging me. Why is she doing that?

Finally, I'm only getting breakfast and dinner these days. What the heck happened to LUNCH? I notice that Marianne still eats lunch every day. And why does she give me such stingy portions? I could eat lots more than the three and a half cups a day I'm getting now. I bet I could polish off the whole bin of kibble, if she'd put it on the floor!

Chow (less than I'd like) for now,
Parker

Dear Parker,

Oh, to be a five-month-old puppy again--I well-remember your angst, especially about food.

But let's talk about rules as they pertain to working dogs. Sitting on the couch is allowed for keeper dogs, not puppies in training. That's why you are told *off* and they are not. Now, this doesn't mean you will never get to sit on the on the couch or the bed. But that's up to your graduate partner, not you.

Here's why: your partner may have a condition that makes her body fragile, and big old goofy Parker jumping on the bed might do more harm than good.

You will have to learn to jump up *gently* if you are allowed to snuggle on the bed or the couch, and not launch yourself like a missile from across the room! (You think I don't remember what it's like to have the "puppy zips"? I heard about the recent incident with Marianne's full coffee cup, one very surprised cat, and the drenched couch. *Bad* puppy.)

As for *sit*, the fact that you do it on command is fine, in fact it's great! However, you must sit the *first* time you hear the command, not the fourth time. The command is *sit*, not *sit sit sit sit*. Teenage stubbornness is uncool.

Remember, you're learning to be a service dog, possibly helping someone in a wheelchair, so where you sit is as important as sitting on command. Marianne wants you to sit next to her, with your ear flap right next to her leg. The only exception is when you learn *front*, which means to sit facing Marianne, directly in front of her. Being in the right position will be helpful later on when you learn *side* and *heel*.

Finally, let's talk about food. O Poor Starving Puppy, I've made up a haiku just for you:

> *Ghosts of Kibble Past*
> *Ghosts of Kibble Yet to Be*
> *Haunt hungry puppy*

You are being just a bit melodramatic, aren't you? Don't you still get training treats during the day? And don't you usually get a stuffed Kong in the morning while Marianne reads the paper? Right, I thought so.

But I feel your pain. All the Canine Companions dogs (and most pet dogs) start with three meals a day because puppies have small tummies. But now that you are older and more grown up you can have more food for breakfast and dinner, so no need for lunch.

Wait—I can already hear you whining that you'd like more food and three meals. No go, buddy. Sorry. Marianne promised that she'd keep you fit and slender. Why, you ask?

Well, it's not just about your good looks. In fact, it's really not about that at all. You need to be in good shape so you have the energy it takes to be a working dog. Also, fat dogs don't live as long. Trim dogs live about fifteen percent longer, and for us Labs that's two years!

Not only does Canine Companions want you to live a long and happy life just because you are such a splendid dog, it's important to your future partner. Over the course of a lifetime a disabled person may have several service dogs. If each dog is kept trim and healthy, that person may need one or two fewer dogs total. Think about the implications of that, my friend!

OK, OK, no more lecturing. You are a growing puppy, so I'll tell Marianne you're ready for more food at breakfast and dinner. Maybe she'll give you a few more carrots in your Kong, too.

Love,
Labby

CELL DOG

I made a new (very large) friend this week! Camden came to stay with us for a few days on his way to professional training in Oceanside. I thought I'd try out my reporter skills again and interview him.

PARKER: Wow, you're really big! I weigh almost fifty pounds, but I feel like a Chihuahua next to you.

CAMDEN: Yeah, I'm told I'm the spittin' image of my handsome dad, Baumann, including his giant blocky head. I am a full Lab, and I weigh about eighty-five pounds. I don't know why that means I can't be a good lap dog, though. I love hugs.

PARKER: Marianne didn't seem to mind when you climbed into her lap so she could hug you. I'm a little jealous of all the attention you got this week.

CAMDEN: *eyeroll* Don't worry. I'm sure everyone still loves you best.

PARKER: Marianne says your puppy-raising experience is different than mine. What's she talking about?

CAMDEN: I was raised by some inmates at a prison called Kit Carson Correctional Center—that's KCCC—in Burlington, Colorado, along with seven other pups. Six dogs are still there, and my buddy Duvall is going to professional training with me on Saturday. Maybe we'll be roommates!

PARKER: What was KCCC like? How did they decide who would raise you?

CAMDEN: Because Canine Companions pups are so special, it's a really competitive program to get into. The inmates have to live in the Honors Pod and pass a rigorous screening process. We lived in the cells with our raisers, slept in crates at night (just like you do), and went to different places in the prison during the day.

PARKER: Huh, that's interesting. But why raise puppies in a prison?

CAMDEN: Why not? Just like other puppy raisers, the inmates want to do something good for someone else. This is a way they can give something back to society. And we got great care, lots of love, and really good training.

PARKER: What about lots of toys and playtime? Was it all work and no play? I'd really miss those things!

CAMDEN: Well, of course we had toys and playtime, you silly goof! We're puppies, after all. We played with our raisers and the pups had playtime together every day. Although *cough* I'm embarrassed to admit that I'm not allowed soft toys because I have a terrible habit of tearing them to pieces. I just can't seem to stop myself from ripping the stuffing out of them. But I love tennis balls, Kongs, and chewie bones.

PARKER: Ah, I wondered why Marianne put all of our soft toys away this week. I guess we'll have to play fetch with tennis balls while you're here. Did you have puppy class twice a month like I do?

CAMDEN: We had classes like yours, but our Canine Companions contract trainer came out only once a month to work with us and our raisers. However, we had a class EVERY DAY with our puppy raisers! That's why I know my commands so well. *YAWN* Professional training is going to be a snap for Duvall and me.

PARKER: I heard that a lot of the pups before you graduated, true?

CAMDEN: Yes, the first group of seven pups had five graduates, which is <u>excellent</u>. Our puppy raisers were so proud of them! Duvall and I are going to try to follow in their paw prints.

PARKER: I heard Marianne say you might follow another career path, like your dad. What's she mean by that?

CAMDEN: Oh, that. Um ... well ... I'm extra-special because I might get chosen for the Canine Companions breeder program. I'm not completely sure what that means—something about going to the Northwest campus for "dates" with the breeder girls. It sounds like fun, but I'll have to wait and see if I pass the health and temperament tests.

PARKER: Hey, Baumann was Hudson's dad too, so you're half-brothers! Marianne says only the best of the best get picked for the breeding program. If you're chosen, maybe Marianne will get to raise a Camden puppy someday.

CAMDEN: Wow, that would be cool! Maybe the inmates would get one of my puppies to raise, too.

PARKER: I get to go lots of places with Marianne. What about you? Did you get to go places besides the prison? You seem really confident.

CAMDEN: Yes, the prison staff took us out to restaurants, shopping, movies and stuff like that. And sometimes we went home with them on overnights. It was fun!

PARKER: The Denver puppy raisers say it takes a village to raise a puppy, so I guess everyone at the prison was your village, just like everyone at 7News is part of my village. Good luck at professional training!

CAMDEN: Thanks! I'll let you know how it goes.

[Happy ending: Camden did indeed get chosen as a breeder.]

Chow for now!
Parker

FIRST AID FOR PETS

You know that September is National Preparedness Month, right? And you're ready for emergencies of all kinds, right? But did you ever think about emergency preparedness for your pets? Huh? DID YOU??

I thought not. Good thing the American Red Cross does think of these things. Marianne and I recently took a Pet First Aid class, and she's now OFFICIALLY CERTIFIED in Pet First Aid. Whew. It's a relief for all of us at home, let me tell you.

I was a little scared when we walked into the classroom, because there were a bunch of lifeless dogs and cats lying on the floor.

"WHAT HAVE YOU DONE TO MY FRIENDS?" I cried.

Marianne patted me and whispered "They aren't real, they are pretend animals. You'll see why."

I sniffed around a bit and realized she was right, they weren't real, but I still didn't understand why they were there. To be honest, it was a little creepy.

But once class started I figured it out. Turns out you can do CPR on a pet, just like you can on a human! Only instead of calling it mouth-to-mouth, it's called mouth-to-snout. *SNORT* That made me laugh out loud.

Anyhow, the pretend animals are for the humans in class to practice on. This class was really lucky because they also had ME to practice on. Marianne made me lie on my right side, and she carefully positioned my head, and then she used a funny-smelling plastic barrier over my snout while she gently blew air in. It tickled, but I was a good boy and lay still, pretending to be hurt. I didn't even wag my tail. Much.

Besides CPR, we learned about other emergencies, like what to do if the pet eats poison (YUCK), or gets bitten by a snake (EWWW), or needs a bandage (OUCH).

I napped through a lot of it, but Marianne woke me so she could practice the Heimlich Maneuver. I feel confident that if I accidentally swallow a ball, she'll help me cough it up. OOOF.

The class practiced bandaging the fake animals, and some of them practiced on me, too. One nice lady did such a good job of bandaging my paw that I limped around the room so everyone could admire it. I'm quite a good method actor.

Chow for now!
Parker

BREEDER GIRL VELVET

After chatting with Camden I was curious about Canine Companions' excellent breeding program. I decided to ask breeder dog Velvet about the program.

PARKER: How did you get chosen to be a Canine Companions breeder dog? I don't mean to sound rude, but what made you so special?

VELVET: Jeez, that does sound rude. But I know what you're getting at. When I started at professional training, the trainers were impressed with my mad skills, so they gave me extra tests to see if I had the right stuff to be a breeder. You have to really know your commands, have a very reliable, steady personality, and be very healthy to be chosen as a breeder. Canine Companions has extremely high standards because it's a very, very important job. They want to pass on the very best traits to the puppies in the program.

PARKER: So you're the "best of the best?"

VELVET (modestly): Yes, I guess I am.

PARKER: Where do you live now? Are you with your puppy raisers?

VELVET: I live with my breeder caretakers, Carol and Dave. All the breeder dogs have to live within a certain distance from headquarters in Santa Rosa, California, so that it's easy for the breeder caretakers to get them to Canine Companions when they are needed.

PARKER: How many litters of puppies have you had? Where are they now?

VELVET: So far I've had two litters of puppies. I had seven puppies (the "P" litter) the first time, and eleven the second time (the "T" litter)! That was a lot of work, keeping eighteen babies happy and healthy. My pups are now all over the country, in Maryland, Colorado, California, Georgia, Ohio, Oregon, and Florida.

PARKER: What happens after the puppies are born? How long do they stay with you at home?

VELVET: Whew! There is a lot of work involved during the eight weeks they are with us until they go to their puppy raisers. I often hear Carol tell people that it's just like caring for human infants. I have to clean them, feed them, and keep them warm because they are unable to regulate their own body temperatures.

Carol and Dave's jobs include weighing the puppies twice a day for the first week to make sure they are gaining weight (then four times a week after that); making sure our whelping room is kept at a comfortable temperature and is quiet; maintaining a clean area for the puppies (you have no idea how hard this is!); providing lots of human contact and appropriate stimulation to help the babies develop; trimming their nails; and taking lots and lots of photographs!

PARKER: Wow, I didn't know it was that complicated. I just remember playing a lot with my brothers and sisters. I guess we were a lot of work!

VELVET: You have no idea!

PARKER: I heard that puppies are blind and deaf at birth, but that can't be right, can it?

VELVET: Yup, it sure is. Puppies' eyes start opening into little slits about day ten, and then fully open a couple of days after that. They still can't see very well—everything is really fuzzy until the muscles in their eyes learn how to work. We keep the lights in the whelping room low so that it doesn't hurt their eyes.

Their ears are totally closed the first three weeks and then gradually began to open. We have to be very careful with noises during this time so that the puppies are not startled. No vacuuming, doorbells, loud TV, or slamming doors, because we don't want any of the puppies to associate loud noises and fear.

PARKER: I guess my breeder caretaker did the same thing, because I'm not bothered by any noises. Hey, Marianne showed me a photo of the puppies. What's up with the yarn collars?

VELVET: It helps us tell them apart. We also use a bit of non-toxic paint right above their tails in case the yarn comes off. Each puppy is assigned a color as soon as it is born and the color order is always the same for Canine Companions pups, according to the birth order: red, blue, purple, neon green, neon pink, brown, light pink, turquoise, orange, and dark green.

PARKER: Hey, my baby collar was brown so I was the sixth puppy in my litter! What happens if the collars come off? I remember we chewed on each other's collars, and sometimes they fell off.

VELVET: If the puppy looses the yarn collar and the paint also comes off, we have other ways to tell who is who, such as their weight, and the personality or physical traits we have observed. Carol checks yarn collars FREQUENTLY just to be safe!

PARKER: When do the puppies start eating kibble? I remember having lots of fun with my siblings when we first got "real" food! We made a huge mess, as I recall.

VELVET: We wean the pups around four weeks, thank Dog! Sadly, this is also when my meals become a lot smaller. When I'm nursing puppies, I eat about eleven cups of food per day. The puppies don't start eating dry kibble right away. Carol makes it really mushy for them for about a week and gradually decreases the water she puts in it. At first they walk in the dishes and wear almost half of what we feed them. It's fun for me to go back into their pen after their meals and lick the food off them!

PARKER: I've heard people ask Marianne if we're evaluated when we're tiny puppies.

VELVET: Breeder caretakers do several "exercises" with the babies. These start very early in the puppies' lives, usually within the first week! The first exercise each breeder caretaker does determines stamina and nursing instinct. Carol places a towel on the floor with eighteen inches marked on it. Then she places a puppy at the starting line and cups her hand around the puppy's muzzle so there is a good feeling of contact for the pup. If the nursing reflex is triggered, the puppy will push his way against her hand. Carol measures how far he pushes.

Another exercise takes place when the puppies are six weeks old. Carol takes each puppy to a room away from the rest of the litter and puts it down on the floor facing away from her, and then steps back a couple of steps. She records what the puppy does: freeze, back up, turn around, come right back to Carol, whine, bark, or cry.

PARKER: What if the puppy does the wrong thing? Do they flunk out?

VELVET: There aren't any right or wrong outcomes to the exercises. They just record what each puppy's response is. Canine Companions uses this data as it tracks the puppy for his or her lifetime, so they can track the types of behaviors a graduate dog started out with. It helps them determine which breeder dogs to put together to potentially make the most graduates.

PARKER: They keep track of EVERYTHING, don't they? I guess I'd better mind my manners! Do you miss your puppies when they go to their puppy raisers at eight weeks?

VELVET: Yes and no. I don't miss their sharp little teeth! Carol and Dave don't miss the noise and the endless cleaning. But we do miss the puppies.

PARKER: Will you be a breeder dog forever? How many litters do you think you'll have? Ten?

VELVET: Good grief, I'm not going to have to be a breeder for my whole life! I will be retired by the time I am six years old. Or, if I have five litters of puppies before I am six, I'll be retired then. I'm not a puppy factory!

PARKER: Oh. What's your plan for retirement?

VELVET: When I retire I expect to be able to continue my current activities of sleeping, playing, helping on our farm, and traveling.

Chow for now!
Parker

FIRE!

We've been hearing a lot about wildfires in Southern California and I know many of you are wondering if my fellow Canine Companions dogs (including Hudson!) at professional training in Oceanside are OK. Everyone (including the staff) is fine! WHEW!

Marianne and the other puppy raisers have been receiving frequent updates from our puppy program manager. The staff has a detailed evacuation plan in place, but so far has not needed to use it. They even included Bob, the resident cat, and Zeek and Stu, the resident bunnies, in the plan. (Bob, Stu and Zeek are actually part of the training staff. They run around and try to distract the dogs; talk about difficult training exercises!)

Some of the trainers and kennel staff have been staying on campus around the clock, just in case evacuation becomes necessary. Fortunately, there's a full kitchen and dorm rooms, so they are very comfy. I don't THINK the dogs are sleeping in the dorm rooms on the beds, but I don't know that for sure. Desperate times, desperate measures, and all that. *snicker*

The humans are wearing masks when they are outside because the smoke is so thick. The dogs are all inside in the training rooms, having play time in addition to regular training. After all, Team Training starts very soon. Hudson said he'll tell me more about that as it gets closer.

So don't worry about my friends in Oceanside. Everyone is safe and well-cared-for.

Chow for now!
Parker

HUDSON GOES TO TEAM TRAINING

Marianne is in such a tizzy this week that it was hard for me to get a bark in edgewise. I finally got her to sit down and tell me what was so exciting.

It seems that Hudson has been selected to participate in next week's Team Training! This means that Canine Companions has determined that he's ready to be matched with a partner. WOW! I get it now—pretty heady news!

"Will we know who his person is on Monday?" I asked, wagging my tail excitedly.

"Oh, if only it were that soon," Marianne sighed. "Look, here's an email that tells us what to expect."

It's more complicated than I thought. Here's a summary of what will happen:

Team Training participants (people who have applied for an assistance dog and been approved, and who have been invited to participate in this Team Training class) arrive at the Oceanside campus on Sunday. Team Training officially starts Monday.

Participants work with the trainers and a pretend dog on Monday to learn the commands and how to handle the dogs.

On Tuesday and Wednesday the trainers bring in the dogs that have been selected to participate. There are always more dogs than people, because the trainers want to ensure that every participant receives their perfect match. Dogs that don't make a match are usually held over for the next semester.

After observing how the participants work with the dogs, the trainers will meet to decide which dog to match with each person.

On Thursday the trainers announce the matches. I'm guessing there's a lot of excitement (and maybe some tears of joy) when the people find out which dog has been chosen for them. Then they start working exclusively with their matches, under the careful guidance of the trainers. The match is considered preliminary until the trainers are completely sure the person and the dog are well suited to work together.

Meanwhile, the puppy program manager is calling hopeful puppy raisers who are sitting as close to their phones as possible. Some will be told that their dogs were not matched and will be evaluated the following week to determine what the future holds for them. Other puppy raisers will be told that a preliminary match has been made. Marianne tells me this is puppy raiser code for "Buy a plane ticket—it looks like your dog may graduate!"

The participants work with their dogs through the weekend, which includes an outing to the mall, a sleepover (the dog gets to stay in the dorm room with the person), and one-on-one handling without the trainers.

The graduates describe Team Training as incredibly stressful and difficult. They attend classes during the day and have homework at night. They learn canine behavior theory and how to work with a canine partner, upwards of forty Canine Companions commands, grooming, the finer points of the Americans with Disabilities Act and service dogs, and how to be a safe and effective team. WHEW! Sometimes there are tests during class, and the last day of Team Training includes a public access test at a local mall. Despite all this hard work, participants say it's the best and most rewarding two weeks of their lives.

If all goes well, the puppy raisers will get another call the Tuesday before graduation telling them the match looks good. This is puppy raiser code for "Your dog is going to graduate!"

Of course, after all is said and done, these are dogs. I am the first to admit that we can be goofy, fickle, and sometimes contrary. A dog can be released from the program AT ANY TIME, up to and including graduation (or even afterward, but that's another story). Marianne says she will only believe Hudson is graduating when she sees him on stage with his partner. She has a point: two of her pups have gone through Team Training, not been matched, and then been released. She says she's ready for a graduate dog!

Marianne already has our plane tickets and hotel reservations, so we're going to graduation no matter what Hudson does. But, OH, how wonderful if he makes his perfect match!

Chow for now!
Parker

HUDSON IS GRADUATING!

Last week Marianne and John got THE CALL from Canine Companions telling them that Hudson had made a preliminary match. Much excitement, phone calls to other puppy raisers and friends, and then several days of nail biting while we waited to hear if the match was going to work out.

O frabjous day! Callooh! Callay! Hudson is graduating on Saturday!

At first I didn't know what was going on. There I was, napping by Marianne's desk Wednesday when the phone rang. When Marianne hung up she put her head down on her desk and sobbed.

"What is it?" I cried as I scrambled over to her. "Are you hurt? Who died?" I was terrified.

"No, no," Marianne sniffled as she patted me. "Sorry to scare you. That was wonderful news! Hudson has been matched with his forever person and is graduating. These are happy tears."

Happy tears? I'll never understand humans.

I went back to my nap, and Marianne made about a zillion phone calls. More tears.

"I don't understand why you're so excited," I said. "Canine Companions dogs graduate all the time, right?"

"No, only about thirty-five percent graduate," Marianne explained.

Oh. Now I get it. Yes, this is a big deal.

I decided to put on my 7News Canine Correspondent hat. Vanessa and Kevin, whose pup Phlox is also graduating on Saturday, and Marianne agreed to a group interview.

PARKER: Did you always know that Hudson and Phlox would graduate?

VANESSA: I did! Phlox always enjoyed working and I remember the first few weeks we had her I kept telling her she was the perfect puppy.

MARIANNE: Well, we hoped Hudson would do well. He was an easygoing puppy, very smart, and he liked working. He had a few fear issues, but it seems that he's grown out of them.

KEVIN: Don't say "graduate" too loud. We puppy raisers are a bit superstitious about this topic. It's like talking about a no-hitter in baseball in the sixth inning. Seriously, I don't know if I will believe it until they call Phlox's name and we hand over her leash. Now saying this, I always believed she was suited for this work. Our backup plan always included her working in some capacity. So there was always hope.

PARKER: What do you know about Phlox and Hudson's new partners?

VANESSA: Phlox has been matched with a gentleman who is a paraplegic. He is very active and plays wheelchair tennis. He wanted a dog so he could have more independence and also have someone to fetch his tennis balls during practice! That is Phlox's dream job. He is from Denver, which is really amazing considering our region serves eight states.

MARIANNE: Hudson has been matched with a young woman from Texas. She is seventeen, attends high school, and her hobbies include photography, painting and drawing, and going to concerts. This is Hudson's dream job too, because he *loves* women and flirts outrageously with them, especially teenagers. I can't imagine a better life for him.

PARKER: What emotions are you feeling right now?

KEVIN: Well, it's a strange mix. It's awesome that Phlox is going to be in the Denver area. My hope is that we can stay in touch with her family. Vanessa and I are so, so proud of her. Another part of my brain is still coming to grips with how this special dog is never going to be "our dog" again. So, in an odd way, I am going through a bit of a grieving period.

I can tell you that when Canine Companions called on Wednesday and told us the great news, I was speechless. Then I wanted to call all of our family and friends! I felt the same way right after Vanessa accepted my marriage proposal.

VANESSA: I am so excited! While I was confident Phlox would end up in the right job with the right person, I feel like her match is one made in heaven. I'm excited to meet "her guy" and see all the new skills she's learned.

PARKER: Is this your first dog to graduate?

MARIANNE: Yes. Trevin and Rolly both went all the way through Team Training before being released after deciding they didn't really want to be 24/7 working dogs. Both are part-time therapy dogs, though. Stryker was released early in professional training for resistance to correction, high prey drive, and low work ethic. He was a great dog, but totally unsuited for service.

KEVIN & VANESSA: Yes. Our first dog, Chisum, was released from the program before turn-in for a medical condition. He is now our "change of career" dog.

PARKER: I know a lot about Hudson, but what makes Phlox special?

KEVIN: That's a tough question. Every Canine Companions dog is special. Some are easier to love right way than others. Chisum was an extremely difficult puppy in that he had his own opinions about proper puppy behavior and he wasn't afraid to share them! Phlox was the complete opposite. She really wanted to please, but in a different way. She wanted approval in her work. What I miss about Phlox is that she was a Velcro dog. Wherever we sat down, she was right at our feet.

VANESSA: "Special" is exactly how everyone who met her described her. She has a very sweet way about her but also has a great balance of enjoying work and enjoying play.

PARKER: Is there anything else you'd like to add?

KEVIN: It's not uncommon for random people to come up to us and say very kind words about what we do as puppy raisers, but I feel that we are the lucky ones. We get to meet such beautiful, smart animals and have them live with us for a period of their life. Because of Canine Companions, I get the opportunity to talk to people that I would probably never meet otherwise. And on Saturday, I will get to share in the true miracle that is Phlox working with her new partner. We are so proud of Phlox and grateful to her for giving us the opportunity to be a part of enhancing someone else's life.

MARIANNE & VANESSA: Sniffle, sniffle, sniffle.

Pass the tissues, and Chow for now!
Parker

HUDSON'S PERFECT MATCH

Marianne says she has her own version of that MasterCard ad:

> *Dog food: $350*
> *Dog toys, treats, crates and accessories: $450*
> *Vet bills: $700*
> *Travel expenses for the weekend in Oceanside: $1,000*
> *Watching Hudson graduate: PRICELESS*

What a weekend! I finally understand what my puppy training is leading up to.

First of all, the Canine Companions trainers are so cool! They all told Marianne that Hudson was the best dog EVER, that they loved him BEST, and he made the best match EVER! (I heard a rumor that they said the same thing to all the other puppy raisers and grads about their dogs, but I'm sure in Hudson's case it was true.)

Second, Hudson looked magnificent in the real working dog blue cape. He kept bragging, "Look, I'm in a REAL cape! I'm GRADUATING today! Aren't I wonderful? Isn't Hilary great?"

Third, Hilary, Hudson's partner, is beautiful and funny and smart and, boy, is he going to have fun with her. Her Mom and sister were there too, and they also said Hudson was the best dog EVER. I think they meant it.

Hilary walks with a cane most of the time but sometimes uses a wheelchair. Hudson helps steady her, picks up her cane when she drops it, and even acts as a brace if she falls. He opens doors, acts as a buffer in crowds to keep Hilary from falling, and fetches anything she needs.

Marianne said her favorite parts of the day were meeting Hilary and her family and getting to know them a little bit, handing the leash to Hilary during the ceremony, and watching Hudson and Hilary working together afterwards.

The parts I liked best were the video of the graduates talking about Team Training, because Hilary made everybody laugh when she talked about working with Hudson, and watching Marianne and John hand Hudson's leash to Hilary on the stage. Even I could see the joy in that moment.

Afterwards, Marianne whispered to me, "I want to do this again, Parker!" I guess she means with me, huh?

Chow for now!
Parker

PETS ARE GOOD MEDICINE

Hospitals can be scary places, especially for kids. But The Children's Hospital here in Denver has a Prescription Pet Program that uses DOGS as medicine! I ask you, what could be better?

I went to The Children's Hospital where I met a Golden Retriever named Tiger, and his human named Adam. They have been involved in the program for five years. They had to be specially trained and pass a "vigorous screening process" by a veterinarian with the Denver Area Veterinary Medical Society, which sounds kind of hard. But I met Sara Mark, the vet who evaluated Tiger at the new hospital, and she was really nice. Tiger said Adam was more nervous about the evaluation than he was!

Tiger and Adam go to the hospital twice a month. Tiger visits kids in the lobby, their rooms, and some of the other areas of the hospital. Adam says they stay as long as needed to make the child feel better. I can tell that just petting Tiger would make most kids feel better. Tiger says he tries to send as much love as he can, and he can tell the kids love him right back. Sometimes it's the patients' families that need the love, and Tiger helps with that as well.

Tiger says the staff at the hospital is super nice, and they tell him they enjoy his visits, too! I was a little jealous because I can tell that Tiger gets a lot of hugs and attention. Marianne told me to get over myself—it's not always all about me. Huh.

The program is so popular that there's a waiting list of people who want to volunteer with their dogs. Give your dog a hug today—it's just good medicine!

Chow for now!
Parker

'TWAS THE NIGHT BEFORE CHRISTMAS REVISITED

This week I was thinking about all the animals at shelters hoping they find forever homes with loving families. While I was pondering this I came up with a poem, which I offer for your entertainment.

Oh, and if you can't think of a present for someone, a donation to a favorite charity or animal shelter is ALWAYS a good choice. Merry Christmas!

'Twas the Night Before Christmas
by Parker (with apologies to Clement Moore)

*'Twas the night before Christmas and all through
the shelter*
The puppies were sleeping in piles helter-skelter.
The kittens were snuggled up together in pairs
*Their fur all fluffed up so they resembled small
bears.*
The bunnies, snakes, gerbils, and rats
Slept blissfully unaware of the cats.
Old dogs slept curled on the worn cement floor
With one wary eye keeping watch on the door.
When suddenly loud noises shook them awake;
A THUMP overhead and the SCREECH of brakes.
Was that someone stomping around on the roof?
A nervous young beagle responded with WOOF!
*The front door opened slowly and who should
appear?*
Why Santa himself, and one curious reindeer.

"You're coming with me!" Santa declared quite
    emphatically.
"Rudolph will sort you into groups
    systematically."
Rudolph consulted a list as he sorted,
While excited young bunnies leaped and cavorted.
"Here Reggie and Blue, Rowdy, Wyatt, and
    Mugsy;
Now Sasha and Stephan, Lucy and Bugsy!"
Rudolph took a deep breath and called out more
    names:
"Norman, Willow, Tribble, Daryl and James."
The animals joyfully jumped in the sleigh
And arranged themselves comfortably out of the
    way.
"The shelter is empty; it's time to get going,"
Said Santa to Rudolph, whose nose was now
    glowing.
The sleigh took off smoothly and soon was in flight
Speeding along through the cold silent night.
"Santa, where are you taking us?" squeaked a silly
    Min Pin.
"You're on your way home now," Santa smiled,
    scratching his chin.
And then each grateful animal was transported
    below
To welcoming homes decorated with lights all
    aglow.
Santa exclaimed as he flew out of sight,
"Happy Christmas to all, and remember, DON'T
    BITE."

Chow for Now!
Parker

PARKER PONDERS THE NEW YEAR

Party, party, party.

Mercy me. The humans have been celebrating what Marianne calls The Silly Season. She explained that at this time of year they eat too much yummy food (a concept I frankly don't understand since all food is yummy and never "too much"), drink festive concoctions, and spend lots of time laughing with friends and family.

I've been to a number of these gatherings recently, and while I don't always get the jokes, I do enjoy being around lots of humans who make a fuss over me and give me belly rubs.

Also, I've noticed that the humans tend to be distracted and not notice when a dog swipes a tidbit or two off the buffet. Not ME, of course, that wouldn't be acceptable service dog behavior, but my sister Madeleine the Greyhound is tall, sneaky, and always on the lookout for snacks. She loves parties.

At any rate, we hosted the neighborhood New Year's Eve party last night and there was much merriment, lots of food and festive beverages. Madeleine got herself banished to the bedroom for surfing the buffet table, but I kept a low profile and munched on too many

Milk-Bones. I guess I got a little silly—I honestly don't remember much—but someone snapped a photo of me wearing a lampshade. How embarrassing.

This morning Marianne was sitting at her desk in the study writing in her new date book. When I asked what she was doing, she explained that humans make resolutions about things they will do in the coming year.

"Like, 'I will eat all my dinner?'" I asked.

Marianne laughed and said, "No silly, we make resolutions about things that will help us improve ourselves. One of my resolutions is to keep my desk tidy."

"Ah," I said, moving away from the edge of the desk as a landslide of books, bills, Christmas cards, and old Canine Companions Newsletters teetered precariously. "I certainly agree with that one. My foot still hurts from *Schulz and Peanuts: A Biography* falling on it yesterday."

"Poor baby," Marianne cooed in a suspiciously mocking tone. I eyed her and she relented.

"No really, I'm sorry," she said. "And that is a good reason why I need to keep the desk tidier. But you could make some resolutions that would help me, too."

"Moi? You mean I'm not the perfect puppy?" I asked in horror.

"Um, well, no, there are things you could work on," Marianne said gently.

And so we worked on our New Year's resolutions together. Here's my list, with a great deal of input from Marianne:

1. I will not remove things from the trash cans. Apparently this is not considered "retrieving."

2. I will not bark at people or other dogs. *Speak* is a command, not an optional activity or performance piece.

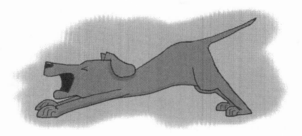

3. I do not need to stretch luxuriously and dramatically every time I get up, even if I do get a laugh from everyone watching. Service dogs are supposed to be unobtrusive. (Huh.)

4. I will lose the teenage attitude and perform a command the FIRST time, not the third time I am asked for it. It turns out she IS the boss of me.

Chow for now!
Parker

Parker's Brother Pilot Checks In

Don't know if you remember, but I have ten brothers and sisters. They are with other Canine Companions puppy raisers all over the United States. Just for fun, I checked in with my brother Pilot to see how he was doing and ask him some questions. He lives with his puppy raiser in Grove City, Ohio.

PARKER: Hi, Pilot! How are you doing? What's it like where you are?

PILOT: We live in a new house (well at least it was new 'til me and my pals tore it up) and we have good neighbors. One of the pictures I sent to you has my neighbor Hannah and me sitting in a lawn chair together. Isn't she cute?

PARKER: Yup, she looks really nice. Who are your pals?

PILOT: They are my adopted "brothers" who live here, too. Jeremy is the oldest. He's thirteen years old, and he's a black Lab. Sagar is also a black Lab, and he's two. They both got kicked out of Canine Companions, so Mom says it's my job to make sure I don't flunk out like they did. I think she's only half kidding!

PARKER: Are they what Marianne calls change of career dogs? Do you get along with them?

PILOT: Yeah, I guess "change of career" is a nicer way to put it. I try to be the boss, but it's kind of hard with an old man and a freak who thinks he's still working. *snicker*

PARKER: What's your puppy raiser like? What kinds of things do you do with her?

PILOT: Roxanne is AWESOME! We do the usual stuff, I guess. I go to church, hand bell choir practice, restaurants, movies, and stuff like that. Nothing too special, but I really like visiting with people.

PARKER: Oh, me too! The best part of going anywhere is having people stop and ask questions about me and give me lots of attention. Of course, they can't pet me when I'm working unless Marianne says they can, but most people know they have to ask. Marianne usually says yes, unless I'm not behaving myself. *cough* Say, what's your favorite toy?

PILOT: Anything with a squeaker in it! I love to run around squeaking it really loud.

PARKER: Yeah, me too! We're a lot alike. What's your favorite command?

PILOT: My favorite command is *up* and my next favorite is *release*. That is how I get to eat!!

PARKER: Oh, yeah—FOOD. *sigh* Say, I have a couple of questions for your puppy raiser. Roxanne, what are some of Pilot's quirks?

ROXANNE: Pilot is a funny dog, and one of his worst quirks is putting his front paws up on things. If he's in a chair, that isn't good enough, he has to put his paws up on the back of the chair. If he encounters anything elevated he has to put his paws up. This is a good thing for his training, but he does it even when he's not invited. We're working on that!

PARKER: Uh-oh. What's his best personality trait?

ROXANNE: His best personality trait is JOY. He is the most joyful dog I have ever had and because of that he tends to bring joy to my life and other people he meets. This is so different from the last dog I raised, Sagar, who was an old soul the day he was born.

PARKER: Marianne says Pilot sounds like her third puppy, Jolly Rolly, and Sagar sounds like her first puppy, Trevin. Me, I'm just a happy boy who loves the spotlight! When does Pilot go to professional training?

ROXANNE: Pilot goes to professional training in May. We live close to the North Central Canine Companions campus, so it's not too far from home. When will you go?

PARKER: I go to the Southwest Campus in Oceanside in August. Hey, Pilot and Roxanne, thanks for talking to me.

PILOT: Bark at ya later!

[Happy ending: Pilot graduated as a Skilled Companion in November 2008.]

Chow for now!
Parker

BRRRRRRR!

Bow wow WOW! Holy Snowman, Underdog, it is COLD outside. Brrrrr.

You may remember that I complained ... er ... wrote about the heat last summer. I thought summer heat was bad enough, but this winter stuff may be even worse.

My feet were so cold on a recent walk that I curled up in a little ball and refused to walk any farther. OK, OK, I wasn't really suffering that much. I was acting a teensy bit over-dramatic, but I wanted to make it clear: IT WAS WAY BEYOND TOO COLD OUTSIDE FOR MAN AND BEAST! Or woman and dog.

At any rate, Marianne got the point because we went home for hot tea (Marianne) and a nap by the fire (me).

However, this ploy of mine rather backfired because Marianne woke me up to put BOOTIES on my paws. Little red booties. Can you imagine the comments from the cats? I was so embarrassed that I hid in my crate for the rest of the evening. Marianne commented on how toasty my paws were when she took the booties off later. Harrumph. They still look silly.

I wondered aloud, "How cold is too cold for dogs to be outside?" Marianne did some research for me. The answer varies a bit, depending on the dog breed. For example, Madeleine the Greyhound needs her fleece coat if the temperature drops below about thirty-five degrees, and she doesn't like to go for walks much longer than twenty minutes. Other dogs with fluffy coats, like Huskies, can tolerate much colder weather.

However, experts feel that anything below ten degrees is too cold for dogs to be left outside, even if they do have cozy, insulated doghouses lined with straw and warm blankets. Here are more cold weather tips:

1. **Please don't leave your dog in your car while you run errands.** In the summer your car becomes an oven and in the winter it becomes a freezer. Dogs can freeze to death if left in a cold car. Trust me, Fido would much rather be home snoozing in his dog bed (or your bed!) than shivering in your car.

2. **Keep your dogs and cats out of your garage or any place they might find antifreeze, which is lethal to pets.** I'm told that it has a sweet taste that is especially appealing to cats.

(Why is Tigger in the garage anyhow, instead of with you in the house? Hmmmm?)

3. **Wipe off your dog's paws, legs, and tummy when he comes in the house.** If you don't, it's possible for him to ingest salt, antifreeze or other chemicals when he licks his paws or legs. Plus, salt can burn our paw pads. OUCH! If you think your dog will tolerate them, booties will protect his paws from cold, chemicals, and ice. Marianne showed me pictures of sled dogs wearing booties, so I guess I'll wear mine after all. Looking silly beats painfully cold paws any day.

4. **Make sure your pets have warm places to sleep, off the floor and away from drafts.** A soft, cozy dog or cat bed with a warm blanket or pillow is ideal, though the couch works just fine too. Now, I'm not saying Madeleine the Greyhound is SPOILED ROTTEN or anything, but Marianne bought her a lovely big papasan chair last week. Since I am not allowed on the furniture, I laugh when I see Madeleine looking wistfully at the cats curled up in HER chair. Ha ha ha.

5. **Be sure your pets have access to fresh water, too.** People forget that water dishes outside can freeze, and we get just as dehydrated in the winter as you do! Also, some dogs need extra protein in the winter if they're exercising a lot.

6. **Finally, keep your dog leashed on walks, especially during snowstorms.** Dogs can lose their scent and easily become lost. I'm told that more dogs are lost during the winter than any other season, so make sure yours always wears ID tags. Actually, that's just good sense any time of the year. In fact, go check your dog's tags right now. Go ahead, I'll wait. Tell me, can you still read the information? If not, splurge and get Fido a new ID tag today.

Chow for now!
Parker

A PAWSOME DOG NAMED HAWK

I keep wondering what I might end up doing after I go to Canine Companions professional training in August, so Marianne suggested I talk to a graduate dog about his job. That sounded like a good idea, so I contacted Hawk, a Canine Companions service dog who lives in California.

PARKER: Where were you raised?

HAWK: I was raised in Texas with a pawsome puppy raiser named Barbara. I was her "Hawkweiller." (She called me that since her other dogs were Rottweilers and I have a head like a Rottweiler.)

PARKER: Pawsome—that's really funny! Um, yeah, your head really is big! Who are your parents?

HAWK: My daddy is Bobby—a very popular breeder for Canine Companions. My momma is Judith.

PARKER: Hey, we're related! Bobby is my great-grandfather on my mother's side. How cool is that? When did you graduate with David? Did you know he was "the one"?

HAWK: We graduated February 2004. I knew he was the one for me when I first met him, but he didn't know it until after the first week, when I finally got to spend a night with him. Shhhh ... don't tell the trainers ... We pups weren't supposed to spend that first night on the bed, but David REALLY needed a full night's sleep, so I got him all comfortable and gave him his first night of sleep in many years! The next morning he was a new person and then he knew I was the one. He saw everything I'd been doing all week for him to make his training easy. I still get to sleep with him to this day. I even pull back the covers for him at night when he says it is bedtime!

PARKER: Wow, that's amazing! Marianne says if I'm really lucky I might get to sleep on the bed when I graduate. What else do you do for David?

HAWK: He's taught me all sorts of ways to help him. He says I know at least 150 ways to help him but (shhh ...) I know more than he realizes! I help David get dressed and undressed, dry his back after baths by pulling on the towel, open doors; turn on lights, pick up things he drops (he's ALWAYS dropping things!), get the phone, hold the refrigerator door, and help him with the dishwasher and laundry. Sometimes, when he's really tired and sore, I pull him around in his wheelchair. I also take things to the different people in our building at work so he doesn't have to push himself so much during the day. I love to work, and he keeps me really busy most days which is so much fun!

PARKER: *GULP* I'm not sure I can learn to do all of those things. You're the Superman of Canine Companions dogs! What's your favorite off-duty activity?

HAWK: SLEEPING!!!

PARKER: Oh, yeah, me too! Do you have any dog pals that you hang out with?

HAWK: I love hanging out with other Canine Companions dogs. Sometimes one of David's co-workers brings his guide dog to work, and I get to play with him on breaks.

David got me a pet cat—she's really cool! She lets me cuddle and we play hide and seek. We also lie on the floor and bat balls around.

PARKER: Everyone thinks dogs and cats don't get along, but that's just silly. I have two cats at home that I hang out with.

Hey, I hear you actually LIKE having your teeth brushed—really?!? How about having your nails trimmed and your ears cleaned? I hate all of it.

HAWK: I LOVE having my teeth brushed! David uses chicken-flavored toothpaste and lets me put my paws up on the sink counter so I can watch him in the mirror and make sure he gets all my teeth! I also love having my ears cleaned—it feels SO good, and then they don't itch, and I don't get a headache shaking my head so much trying to get rid of the itch. I don't really like getting my nails trimmed but I know afterward I'll get a good treat if I behave.

I also love getting brushed—it feels doggone good, especially after a bath! David has a bathtub especially for me, in my own bathroom, and he always gets the water just the right temperature. I'm so nice and shiny when he's done with me, and I get LOTS of attention then!

PARKER: Hmmmm, I can see that Marianne is going to use you as an example the next time she nabs me for grooming. It sounds like you and David have an amazing partnership and lots of fun.

HAWK: I have the best job in the world. Canine Companions put me with a human who loves me and makes sure I'm spoiled! He also makes sure I get to do lots of work, which I love, and he's always willing to teach me new things.

PARKER: Graduation sounds better and better to me, even if it means putting up with getting my teeth brushed.

Chow for now!
Parker

IT'S MY BIRTHDAY AND I'LL BARK IF I WANT TO

HAPPY BIRTHDAY TO ME!

I am a year old! Quite a milestone in anyone's life, and no exception for Canine Companions dogs. My mama, Carie, sent a birthday greeting to us: "Wishing Penela, Patrina, Piute, Pixel, Palmer, Pippi, Peggy, Pasha, Pilot, and Parker a glorious year. My, how you all have grown!"

Mama Carie sent along a few photos of us as tiny pups, and WOW! We really have grown up.

Marianne heard from several of my siblings' puppy raisers. Nancy says, "Palmer goes to work most days with me. I work for a granite company that makes and installs granite countertops. It's dusty but Palmer likes it. He also goes to college with me. I am almost ready to graduate with a degree in interior design, and I've had Canine Companions dogs with me all the way."

I imagine you get extra credit from your teachers if you have a wonderful puppy with you. And even though we look like we're snoozing, we really are listening so we can help with homework, papers, and cramming for exams.

Piute's puppy raiser, Meryl, tells us, "Piute picks up commands quickly and is quite the star in his puppy class. He is spunky, but also cuddly." Marianne says that last part sounds like me!

"And why doesn't the 'star of his puppy class' part apply to me?" I asked.

Marianne eyed me for a minute. "Well, it might if you'd focus a bit more on the commands and less on the possibility of a treat."

Oh.

"Patrina, nicknamed "Trini," is small, very affectionate, and very bright. And did I mention fearless? She loves hiking every weekend and resting in front of the fire on cold winter days. She has stolen my husband's heart and that of everyone else she meets. She is our seventh Canine Companions pup, and her change of career older brother, Doug the Dog, adores her," says Regina. Awwwww!

"Pixel is doing well," says Nancy. "He had a health problem up to about Christmas and since then seems to have outgrown it. He suddenly started packing on muscle and gained ten pounds in the last five weeks. I thought he was going to be relatively small, but now I think he is going to be pretty big!"

Hmmmm. I wonder who is the biggest in our litter. I weigh sixty-seven pounds right now, and Marianne thinks that's as big as I'll get. We'll see!

Finally, a puppy after my own heart, my brother Pilot. "He is a local celebrity due to our participation at a local event called Paws in the Pool" says Roxanne. "The photographer at the event must have liked him because he took a ton of photos!"

Celebrity runs in our family! The Perfect "P" Puppies, that's us.

Chow for now!
Parker

PARKER ASKS THE 64,000 KIBBLE QUESTION

Marianne was filling out my monthly puppy report recently and she told me rather sternly that she was going to call Stu to discuss my little barking problem.

"I don't think it's a problem," I said. "I can stop anytime I want to."

"It *is* a problem," Marianne scolded me. "It's not your job and you need to stop *now*, or I'm enrolling you in a twelve-step program for Barkers Anonymous."

Jeepers. I changed the subject, hoping to divert her. "Who is Stu?"

"Stu Wahrenbrock is the new Southwest Regional Puppy Program Manager. He keeps track of all the puppy raisers and puppies in our region, which includes Arizona, Utah, Colorado, New Mexico, Texas, Oklahoma, Arkansas, Southern California, Southern Nevada, and Hawaii."

"Yow, that's a lot of people and puppies!" I yelped. "He must be really busy. I bet he doesn't have time to worry about a little barking." A thought occurred to me. "Hey, does that mean he's your BOSS?" I couldn't help it; I actually snickered.

"Well, yes, it does," Marianne admitted. "He's the person who decides if we can raise another puppy, and he holds us accountable for the current puppy, which would be *you*. I don't know why you find that so amusing."

I dunno, I guess I was just glad to find out that someone gets to boss Marianne around, since she's always telling me what to do. And not do. Like barking. Bother.

Anyhow, I decided I wanted to talk to Stu and find out more about him and his job.

PARKER: Hey, Stu. What interested you about the position of puppy program manager at Canine Companions?

STU: The Canine Companions program really begins with the puppies and the puppy raisers. Without their love and commitment we wouldn't be able to perform the miracles that we do.

PARKER: Yup, it's all about the puppies, at least in my opinion. How many puppy raisers are in your region? How do you know which puppies go where?

STU: We have about 225 puppy raisers in the Southwest Region. A number of our puppies are named to honor donors or supporters of Canine Companions. When that's the case, I try to place those puppies close to where the donor or supporter lives. In other situations we place puppies where we have available puppy raisers. We have a very complete database that helps.

PARKER: What is your favorite part of your job?

STU: When I watch local puppy raisers see their new Canine Companions puppies for the first time. It is really a special moment.

PARKER: Awww, I bet that is amazing. Marianne says she vividly remembers the first time she saw each of her pups, and she says it's wonderful every single time. What's the hardest part of your job? What is your biggest challenge?

STU: Having to call puppy raisers to tell them that the puppies they raised are being released from the program is the hardest, and continuing to find good puppy raisers is a challenge.

PARKER: What was your biggest surprise about working for Canine Companions?

STU: I knew that the volunteers were at the heart of making Canine Companions work, but I am continually amazed at all they will do for the organization. So many of our volunteers are very successful in their own professions but will drop everything if a major need arises.

PARKER: OK Stu, here's the 64,000 kibble question: When are you going to raise a Canine Companions puppy?

STU: Time will tell. I have two Golden Retrievers now and I'm still trying to learn this job. I do puppy-sit when the need arises.

PARKER: Is there anything else you'd like to tell me?

STU: Canine Companions for Independence is a great organization filled with incredible people, both staff and volunteers. Everyone seems to know why we're here, and they are committed to the mission.

PARKER: I couldn't have said it better myself.

Chow for now!
Parker

TRADED!

One of the peculiar things puppy raisers do is trade pups.

Even Marianne says that if you'd told her before she started puppy raising that she would willingly, nay, cheerfully, hand over her pup's leash to another puppy raiser, she wouldn't have believed you. She recently admitted how peculiar this practice might seem to outsiders when my Auntie Jennifer came to get me for a sleepover. Seems she was in town for the weekend and puppyless, so she called Marianne and asked if I could spend the weekend with her. Within fifteen minutes my bag was packed and we hit the road. I had a wonderful time, too.

Which brings me back to the topic of trades. Marianne asks for trades! She initiates trades! I can't tell if she wants to get rid of me, or get her hot little paws on someone else's puppy, or both.

I was a bit nonplussed last week when I was traded with puppy raisers in Colorado Springs I'd never met before because Marianne wanted to see how I'd do in a "completely new environment."

Huh. Parker as Lab Rat. I feel so ... experimental.

Truth is, I had a fabulous time. At first I worried that maybe Susan and Dave weren't real Canine Companions puppy raisers. Would they know the commands and all the rules? Turns out they've raised lots more pups than Marianne and John, so they not only know all the commands and rules, they know how to deal with super-smart, too-big-for-his-collar pups like me.

So, we had several discussions about inappropriate barking. But on the plus side, we had a ton of fun. They loved the stuffing out of me, and told Marianne, "Parker should toot his own horn about how everyone was so impressed by his quiet demeanor and excellent commands." HA! I repeat, HA!

I asked Oden how he'd fared at my house. He said that he had a great time, but the week was not without its lessons. He said that he learned the following things:

1. Barking at the cats and doing a play bow will not entice them to play, nor are they pleased to have a toy shoved in their faces.

2. Fits of temper in the crate at bedtime are useless.

3. Madeleine the Greyhound does not share toys. Trying to steal a toy when she's dozing will result in a sharp correction. She may be old, but she's still fast!

4. Curling up in John's lap and snoozing quietly for a whole hour while he reads the morning newspaper is a nice way to start the day.

5. However, leaping into Marianne's lap for a cuddle is not a good idea if she has a cup of HOT HOT HOT coffee in her hand at the time. Oden learned some new words, but Marianne told him he was not allowed to repeat them.

Marianne and Susan are planning another trade in a few weeks. Oden and I can't wait!

Chow for now!
Parker

SUCCESSOR DOGS

This morning I found Marianne gift wrapping a small package and humming cheerfully.

"What's that?" I sniffed at it curiously.

"Oh, just a little present for a puppy raiser," she replied.

"Oh," I said. "Someone's birthday?"

"Nope, it's a graduation gift." She finished the bow with a flourish of ribbon. "We're going to the May turn-in and graduation party this weekend, remember?"

I thought about it for a minute and shook my head. "I remember the party, but I'm confused. Graduation is May 31st. I thought we wouldn't know which dogs are graduating until a few days before. Please explain!"

Marianne sat down on the floor with me and cradled me in her lap, rubbing my tummy.

"OK, here's the scoop. You're right about the timing. Team Training begins on Monday. We hope that Denver dog Durango will meet his forever partner in that class. But there are three teams also graduating on May 31st who were matched last month. Canine Companions calls it a side placement when a team is matched outside of the regular Team Training process."

"Why would they do that?" I asked. "I thought Team Training was when the person and dog learned to work together, like Hudson and Hilary."

"That's true," Marianne replied. "But sometimes the person is getting a successor dog and doesn't need the full two-week training course because he or she is more experienced."

"Could you rub my paws?" I asked. "What's a successor dog?"

Marianne gently massaged my front paws. "People get successor dogs after their first dog retires. Just like humans, dogs reach a point when they don't want to work anymore, or can't because they're not physically up to it. Canine Companions helps the graduate determine when it's time to retire a dog, how to make the transition, and how to apply for a successor dog. And since the person has been through Team Training once, the staff may decide that the team can learn to work together in just a few days with the help of a Canine Companions trainer. In this case they held a mini Team Training session on campus for a week in April with three teams."

I sighed happily. I do love a paw massage. "Do you know who the three dogs are?"

Marianne switched to rubbing my back paws. "I do," she said. "One is Therese, who is a successor Service Dog. One is Kirin, who is a successor Skilled Companion. The third is Rosey, a Facility Dog."

"What jobs will they do?" I wondered.

"Therese will help open doors, pick up dropped items, turn on lights, and other tasks to help her person be more independent. Kirin is part of a three-part team of a boy and his parents. She'll help with physical tasks, but she will also act as a social ice-breaker and companion for the boy. Rosey will work with her partner in a veteran's hospital. I don't know exactly what tasks she will do, but I imagine she'll help with physical or occupational therapy in some fashion."

I yawned and stood up. "I bet their puppy raisers are excited. I remember how happy you were when you found out that Hudson was graduating."

Marianne smiled. "Yup. Getting that phone call was one of the best moments of my life." She eyed me thoughtfully for a minute. "You don't suppose I'll get a phone call like that about you, do you?" she inquired politely.

"Wait and see," I said as I walked away. "Wait and see."

Chow for now!
Parker

THE CELEBRATED MR. K

Big excitement around here.

Marianne received a phone call last week from Stu regarding the arrival of Puppy #6 on July 11. I get to be an Assistant Puppy Raiser for a little while!

We know that his mom is named Jennifer and dad is Weldin. There are seven puppies in the litter: four girls and three boys. We're getting one of the boys.

We don't know his name yet. See, Canine Companions names all the pups in a litter with the same first letter and this is a K litter, the so-called Special Ks. My litter was the Perfect Ps. HA!

Anyhow, Canine Companions has a Naming Fairy who chooses the names for the pups. She accepts input from the breeder caretakers and others, but she has ultimate say on the names. Names are not used more than once, unless the currently-named dog retires, is released from the program, or (gulp) dies. I am Parker II, meaning Parker I is no longer in the Canine Companions program.

Marianne has been humming some Beatles song about Mr. Kite, something about "Mr. K. will challenge the world!" and "Mr. K. performs his tricks without a sound," which, according to Marianne, means he's not going to be a loud opinionated boy like me. She wishes.

Not that anyone asked me, but I've been thinking of K names.

- 🐕 Mr. Kite, of course.

- 🐕 Katmandu. (Just because I like the sound of it. Oh, and the idea of Marianne calling "Here Kat," and confusing the kitties.)

- 🐕 Koontz. (For Dean, Gerda and Trixie Koontz, Canine Companions supporters for whom the SW campus is named!)

- 🐕 Kibble. (FOOD ... yum.)

- 🐕 Klinger. (We watch a lot of M*A*S*H reruns around here.)

- 🐕 Kangaroo. (Boing! Boing! Boing!)

- 🐕 King. (What dog doesn't want to be named King?)

- 🐕 Kelpie. (Mischievous water spirit; it would serve Marianne right.)

- 🐕 Klaxon (Loud horn. HAHAHAHA.)

- 🐕 Knickknack (Paddywack. Give the dog a bone.)

Ah, well. Soon enough we'll find out the new puppy's name.

Chow for now!
Parker

STILL THE ONE

Uh-oh.

I have seen the future and his name is KIRBY.

Kirby V, to be exact.

Oh, you should hear the puppy raisers and my co-workers exclaiming over the photos: "He's so cute! He's adorable! He's perfect!"

Blech. Nauseating, really.

I mean, what happened to "Parker, you're so cute!" "You're adorable!" "You're the cutest puppy ever!"

I am still the Cutest, Smartest, Best Puppy in the Whole World, right? Right? Just like the song says, "We're still having fun and I'm still the one!" Right? I said, "RIGHT?!"

After all, I'm housebroken, I don't chew on anything except my approved toys, I'm really well-behaved in public, I can do a *down-stay* like nobody's business, and I know all my commands. Who else does the nifty little spin and flourish when told to *heel*? NO ONE, that's who. HA!

Well, at least I have a few weeks to bask in the glory of being the Cutest Puppy in the World before old what's-his-name gets here.

SIGH

Chow for now!
Parker

PUPPY BREATH

Kirby, Kirby, Kirby!

Only two more weeks and Marianne's next Canine Companions puppy, Kirby, arrives in Denver. "But where is he now?" I wondered. "And who is taking care of him?"

"Silly," Marianne said. "He's in northern California with his mom and siblings, and he's being cared for by his breeder caretakers. "

Oh, right. I knew that.

I contacted the two breeder caretakers who are responsible for Kirby's mom, Jennifer, and her puppies. It sounds like a huge amount of work to me. I asked Pauline and Linda how they felt about the whole experience.

"Despite the constant work, the sleepless nights, and being confined to the house a good bit of the time, we really love it when we have puppies," said Pauline. "Even though Jennifer has puppies right now, I am already starting to get excited about our other breeder Angel's next litter."

Linda said, "At eight weeks I'm usually ready to resume my life without puppies. We spend at least two weeks before whelping and eight weeks with the pups worrying about mom and puppies and making sure everything is perfect for both. This entails time, energy, loss of sleep, and friends to get you through it. Is it worth it? *Absolutely!"*

Pauline added "The other thing I would like people to know is that we couldn't do it without other breeder caretakers being willing to help with the puppy care. Even for two people, this is a lot of work. There is also support from the Canine Companions vet clinic and other breeder caretakers who are willing to give advice when there is a problem."

I'm exhausted just listening to this. I'd better rest up before Kirby gets here, huh?

Chow for now!
Parker

THE DREADED MANILA ENVELOPE

When we got home from work yesterday I headed to the water bowl in the kitchen while Marianne sorted through the mail. She gasped, let out a little scream, and dropped a big manila envelope and some papers on the floor.

Madeleine and Mina came skidding into the kitchen, with Mina shrieking,

"Snake! Snake! Snake!"

Madeleine immediately lifted all four feet off the floor. "Where? Where? Where?"

"Calm down!" Marianne scolded. "Mina, hush! Madeleine, relax, you can put your feet down. There's no snake. You're safe."

All three of us stared at her. I walked over and sniffed the papers. "What was all that about?" I asked. "I'm getting a faint whiff of dog, but nothing to cause alarm."

"Sorry," Marianne said as she picked up the stack of colored papers and stuffed them back into the envelope. "It's an envelope from Canine Companions, but I wasn't thinking when I opened it, so I was caught off guard." Madeleine and Mina rolled their eyes and left the kitchen.

I eyed the envelope suspiciously. "We get stuff from Canine Companions all the time. Why is this any different? Why are your eyes all teary?"

Marianne pulled a tissue out of the box and blew her nose. "This is your turn-in packet. It's the paperwork I need to fill out before you go to professional training. I know you're going in August, but I wasn't expecting the packet so soon. It caught me by surprise, that's all."

Oh, professional training. Scary!

"Well, what do we have to do?" I asked. "That looks like a lot of stuff. Do I have to take tests like the high school kids? What's that one called—the S.I.T.?"

Marianne laughed. "No, you do not have to take a standardized test like the S.A.T."

She pulled the papers back out and shuffled through them. "Well, there's general information about turn-in, like the date and time.

There's a checklist reminding me to forward your veterinarian records and to make sure all your shots are up to date. There's an RSVP form to let Stu know if we'll take the campus tour on Friday and attend the graduation on Saturday. Here's a form for the vet to fill out about your general health. And here's the form for your final puppy progress report."

She paused. "Oh, here's something you'll like. It's a reminder to send at least two photographs for the puppy raiser slide show that will be part of the graduation ceremony."

That got my attention all right. "Oooh, photos! Can we take some new ones? You might not have enough to choose from!"

Marianne snorted. "Since we have about 2,378 photos of you I don't think it will be a problem, but we can take some new ones, too." She reached over and rubbed my ears. "Jeez, it seems like just a few months ago that I filled out these papers for Hudson, and now it's your turn."

We looked at each other.

"Well," Marianne said, "It's still eight weeks away, so let's not do today what we can put off until tomorrow. Let's go play fetch for a while."

Chow for now!
Parker

KIRBY, WE HARDLY KNEW YE

We're a little disappointed around here right now.

Kirby, the next Canine Companions puppy after me, was supposed to arrive this week. But Marianne got a phone call from Stu explaining that Kirby would be delayed while the veterinarians at our national office in Santa Rosa, Calif. checked him out.

The next day Stu called to let us know that Kirby won't be coming to Colorado after all. He has some serious health issues, and the veterinary staff at our national office thought it would be best to keep him there so he could continue receiving superb medical care under their supervision.

Marianne says she certainly understands and supports their decision, but she fell in love with his little furry face in those photos and misses him even though she never met him. Love at first sight works like that.

I've been giving her lots of little kisses, hanging out under her feet even more than usual, and generally comforting her, which she says she appreciates. I am a helper dog, after all.

We have our paws crossed that little Kirby makes a full recovery very soon. He will be placed with a puppy raiser in the Northwest Region so that he's close to the Canine Companions vets who can keep an eye on him. Spare a thought for my friend Kirby and his wonderful breeder caretakers, Linda and Pauline, who are worried about him, would you?

Chow for now!
Parker

DECONTAMINATED DOGGIE

Sometimes Canine Companions dogs and puppy raisers are asked to do unusual things, so when Marianne told me we'd been invited to help with a disaster drill at Parker Adventist Hospital, I wasn't sure what to expect. She told me she wasn't really sure either, which didn't exactly bolster my confidence. I mean, why do something that sounds scary when we could just as easily have stayed home in the nice cool house and watched *Animal Planet*?

"Parker," she scolded, "You can be helpful to the hospital staff today. They need to practice what to do if a person with a service dog needed help in an emergency. Besides, this will be an excellent training opportunity for you, too."

Uh-oh. I didn't like the sound of that. "Excellent training opportunity" is puppy raiser code for "weird new experience you might not like."

"Will there be cookies?" I asked hopefully.

"Yes," she laughed, "I will bring some dog cookies for you and Ren."

I perked up. Things can't be too bad if another Canine Companions puppy and cookies are included.

I watched as she packed a small bag with extra clothes, water, a hat, and towels. I was surprised when she dressed in her swimsuit, then put on the casual clothes she wears to her exercise class.

"Greater love hath no puppy raiser than to agree to appear in public in a swimsuit for a dog-training exercise," she told me.

Whoa. Curiouser and Curiouser.

We motored over to Ren and her puppy raiser Pat's house. I was startled to see Pat dressed in similar casual clothes and a HAT, because Pat never does anything that might muss her hair. This was going to be an interesting day indeed.

Soon we arrived at the hospital and made our way into a conference room for instructions. Ren and I got lots of petting and attention from the staff and volunteers, while Marianne and Pat filled out paperwork. Soon all the pretend victims were wearing big tags around their necks.

"What's that for?" I craned my neck, trying to read Marianne's tag.

"It's my new identity." Marianne pointed. "See, it has my pretend name, 'Ima Glowing,' and all the information the staff will need to treat me when I arrive at the emergency room. It says I am seriously injured and I collapse when I arrive at the ER. I am unable to follow instructions. Oh, I am also diabetic."

"What does it say about me?"

"Nothing. See, that's part of the exercise. The staff will have to figure out what to do with you. We'll pretend you're my medical alert dog since I'm diabetic," Marianne decided.

We proceeded outside and made our way to the ER. Pat had different pretend injuries, so she and Ren waited in another area. Marianne "collapsed" on the sidewalk and closed her eyes. I lay down next to her and put my head on her shoulder, playing the part of Concerned Service Dog. I heard several people say "Awwww, he's so cute! Look, he's worried about her." As I said earlier, I'm a really good method actor.

Soon a nurse rushed over and began taking information off of Marianne's tag. She made a wrist tag and placed Marianne on top of a stiff board. Someone brought me a pan of water, which was very thoughtful because it was hot! Nothing more happened, and I dozed for a while, keeping one eye on Marianne and watching the other victims as they received treatment.

Suddenly there was a flurry of activity. Two nurses came over and lifted Marianne onto a high narrow table with wheels, which I found a little alarming.

"It's just a gurney," Marianne whispered. "It's OK; they need it to move me into the ER."

There was a spirited discussion between the two nurses about what to do with me, and they decided that the situation called for Marianne to go on without me because of her serious injuries.

"It's OK, Parker," Marianne said. "Be a good boy and do what they tell you to do." And then they rushed her gurney around a corner and out of sight.

Huh.

Someone handed my leash to another volunteer for a while, but then he was taken away too. I sat on the sidewalk by myself, watching everyone rushing around. I remembered what Marianne said and stayed put since no one had given me a command to do anything. I was dozing off again when a nurse came over and picked up my leash. "Let's go," she said, and we walked around the corner where I'd last seen Marianne.

To my amazement there was a big white tent with two people in strange puffy gray outfits and masks spraying water on a victim with a hose that was dangling from the ceiling. They were scrubbing and rinsing her just like Marianne does when she gives me a bath.

"I'm getting a bad feeling about this," I muttered.

Sure enough, one of the puffy people grabbed my leash, and next thing I knew I was being hosed down with VERY COLD WATER. Marianne didn't mention this part of the drill! At least when she gives me a bath the water is warm; this was freezing! When they were done the puffy people patted me and said I was a good boy, and a nurse took me into the hospital.

To my relief the nurse took me into a room with several very wet people in swimsuits lying on gurneys, including Marianne! She was very happy to see me, and I wagged my tail and gave her and the girl on the next gurney little kisses. Someone brought over a sheet, and Marianne used it to dry me off a bit.

"What the heck was that all about?" I asked. "Why did we get showers, and why were those people dressed so strangely?"

"They were pretending we'd been exposed to radiation and had to be decontaminated before we could enter the hospital," Marianne whispered. "That's why I had my swimsuit on."

"Jeez, you could have warned a dog," I complained. "That was weird and scary and cold."

"I'm sorry," she said, giving me a hug. "I didn't know they'd wash you, too. But I'm very proud of how well you did!"

Just then a gurney went zipping past with Pat lying down and Ren sitting up, her ears flying in the breeze.

Marianne and I cracked up. "What I wouldn't give for a camera right now!" she exclaimed. "Of course, Pat would never forgive me for taking a picture of her with wet hair and no makeup."

Soon Pat and Ren joined us in the room with all the other volunteer victims. Everyone dried off and got dressed, then trooped back to the conference room for some final paperwork and sack lunches. Marianne gave Ren and me cookies for being such good dogs. I was so exhausted that I slept the rest of the afternoon.

"That was fun," I admitted to Marianne later that evening. "Do you think Ren and I helped the staff figure out what to do when someone shows up with a service dog in the middle of a disaster?"

"Oh, I am sure you two were a huge help," Marianne said. "And think how exciting your puppy report will be this month!"

Chow for now!
Parker

GOOD OLD WHAT'S-HIS-NAME

The puppy has landed!

Meet my "little brother," my successor, Marianne and John's Canine Companions puppy #6: ROSS. He arrived Wednesday morning via Continental Airlines and by all accounts is quite happy to be here. I haven't actually met him yet because I'm having a little one-on-one time with our contract trainer, Amy. I'm getting a few extra lessons to help me when I go to professional training next month. But Marianne called to fill me in on the news.

Now I know some of you are as confused as I was when Marianne told me Ross was here. HUH? Who?

You may remember that Kirby, the puppy we were originally expecting, was ill and Canine Companions decided to keep him at the Northwest campus for medical care. His illness is serious enough that he's been released from the program, but the veterinarian who is taking care of him has adopted him! That's good news for everyone.

Stu called to let Marianne know that she and John would be getting a puppy named Tate on Wednesday, July 23rd. Everyone was eagerly awaiting his arrival, until Tuesday afternoon when Marianne got another call from Stu. It seems that, during the routine medical exam that Canine Companions performs an all the eight-week-old puppies before they are sent to their puppy raisers, the vets discovered that Tate had a pronounced overbite.

"Huh?" I said to Marianne. "What do his teeth have to do with anything?"

"Well, it's not an issue for a pet dog, but the trainers and the vets examined him and determined that it would hinder him in picking up many of the objects working dogs are expected to retrieve. Things like keys or credit cards or pens would be hard for him to grasp in his teeth."

Ah, that makes sense. A large part of an assistance dog's job consists of retrieving and carrying items. I guess teeth have a lot to do with a working dog's job, so I'll stop protesting when Marianne brushes mine.

Anyhow, Tate has also been released from Canine Companions and will be adopted as a pet. Marianne hardly had time to absorb this news when Stu said he had another puppy that could come to Denver on Wednesday on the same flight as Tate was supposed to be on, which is how we ended up with Ross. He's a black Lab, and has the same father (Baumann) as Hudson. Marianne was delighted.

"I don't think I could have waited another two weeks for the next 'possible' puppy!" she confided. "It's a relief to have Ross safe and sound on the ground in Denver."

It's not unheard of for things to change with puppies at any stage of the process, but even so, Marianne says this is fairly unusual. If you can imagine such a thing, people were actually suggesting that I was hexing things. Harrumph. I've never been so insulted in all my life. What kind of puppy do they think I am? Marianne told me to lighten up, that people were JOKING.

Oh. Some of that famous puppy raiser humor. Ha ha.

At any rate, Canine Companions has a very carefully monitored breeding program, and having puppies released for health reasons, especially so young, doesn't happen often. Around 950 puppies are born each year to the breeder dogs, so things like this do happen occasionally, but it's just a weird twist of fate that it happened to Marianne and John TWICE IN A ROW.

Marianne said this just proves what Val Valentine, the puppy program manager before Stu, always told the puppy raisers: "Don't get the towels monogrammed until you have the puppy in your arms." Marianne explained that Val meant a puppy raiser shouldn't overdo things for a new puppy until it is in the puppy raiser's home. For instance, she didn't make name tags for Kirby, Tate—or Ross, until now.

"I'll go to the store on Saturday and get a name tag made for Ross," she promised. "I'll probably get him a new toy, too. And yes, Parker, I will get something for you!"

Ross is going to work with Marianne today. I'm a little worried that everyone will forget about me in the hullabaloo a new puppy creates. I'm still The Cutest Puppy in the World, after all.

Chow for now!
Parker

PUPPY OLYMPICS

We've been watching the Olympics at my house. Other than the swimming, which does look fun, I haven't been too interested. But as I watched Marianne leap over the baby gate, with eleven-week-old Ross in her arms, headed for the back door at top speed, it seemed to me that she was competing in some sort of Olympic Games herself.

"Why, yes," she laughed when I mentioned it. "In fact, when we had Rolly as a puppy in 2004, I wrote a little piece about the Puppy Olympics. Let me see if I can find it."

Sure enough, she found it later that evening. She said that puppy raisers Cath and Vanessa also contributed to the list of events. For your amusement I present THE PUPPY OLYMPICS!

- **100 Meter Dash (Home):** Scoop up squatting puppy and make a mad dash for the back door.

- **200 Meter Dash (Work):** Scoop up squatting puppy and dash for the nearest exit. Points deducted if you forget to grab your security badge and a poop bag.

- **Hurdles:** Scoop up squatting puppy, jump over the baby gate and run for the back door.

- **Weight Lifting:** Pick up the puppy. Pick up the puppy. Pick up the puppy. Pick up the puppy. Pick up the puppy.

- **Gymnastics:** Prepare dinner and clean up kitchen while dodging puppy, other dogs, and assorted puppy toys scattered over the kitchen floor.

- **Synchronized Swimming:** Give squirming, gleeful puppy a bath and get drenched in the process.

- **Softball:** Throw the ball for the puppy. Throw the ball for the puppy. Throw the ball for the puppy. Fetch the ball yourself.

- **Marathon:** Stand at the end of the leash and say hurry. Pull leaf/stick/twig/rock out of the puppy's mouth. Repeat endlessly until the puppy hurries. Extra points awarded for 2 a.m. start time or severe weather.

- **Wrestling:** Dress wiggling puppy in his baby cape (which ties around the neck and under his tummy) and Gentle Leader head collar. Points deducted if the puppy unties one set of cape ties before you get the other set tied and/or paws the Gentle Leader off his nose.

- **Shot Put:** Throw a shoe at the crate to quiet the whining puppy so you can get at least four consecutive hours of sleep. Extra points awarded for actually hitting the crate in the dark. If the event takes place near a water hazard, points deducted if the shoe falls into the water dish after hitting the crate.

- **Long Jump:** Leap across the room in a single bound to snatch contraband item from puppy. Extra points awarded if you don't get stabbed by tiny puppy teeth in the process. Style points awarded if you can continue your conversation with your spouse or co-worker while executing the jump.

- **Shooting:** Without hitting the cat, squirt the puppy with vinegar water to discourage playful pouncing on the kitty.

- **Puppy Pentathlon:** A day in the life of a puppy raiser! Includes a minimum of ten hurry breaks (at least one between the hours of midnight and 5 a.m.), scooping poop at least four times, removing twenty forbidden items from the puppy's mouth, preparing three meals, giving the puppy one bath, squirting the puppy six times for chasing the kitty, wrestling puppy into his cape and Gentle Leader twice, and cuddling the puppy for a minimum of an hour.

Chow for now!
Parker

SMILE

We were driving to work this morning when a sappy old song came on the radio, lots of violins and some guy crooning on about smiling even though hearts are breaking and clouds are in the sky and smiling through tears and treacly stuff like that. We pulled into the parking lot as the song ended.

I sat up. "Jeez, that was a sappy song," I commented. Marianne sat in front seat, not moving. "Hey, let's go." I said. "We're gonna be late to the morning meeting." I heard a funny noise so I peered over the seat at her. "Are you crying?" I asked. "You are! You're crying! Why? What's wrong?"

"I am not crying," Marianne said as she snatched up a tissue and blew her nose. "Nope, not me, huh-uh. You must be mistaken. I have allergies."

"Yeah, allergies, sure," I scoffed. We got out of the car and headed into the station to our office. "Really, tell me the truth—why are you sad today?"

She sighed loudly, closed the door to the office and sat down. "OK, you're right, I am a little sad today because this is your last day at work. We fly to California tomorrow to take you to Canine Companions professional training, remember?"

"Well, sure," I said, puzzled. "You told me all about professional training. Sounds like fun to me."

"That's right," Marianne said, pulling me into her lap in my favorite cradle position. She hugged me. "Oh Parker, you are going to have such a good time. The trainers and kennel staff will love you to pieces and you'll get to play with the other dogs a couple of times a day, and go on field trips, and learn to do amazing things."

I craned my head around and eyed her suspiciously. "So if going to professional training is such a great thing for me, why are you all teary again?"

She gave me a watery smile. "Some humans cry when we're happy or sad, and turn-in is always a bit of both for me. I'm so proud of you and I am going to miss you." She put me down and grabbed another tissue. "I'm just having my usual epiphany. See, with each puppy there's one moment when I suddenly realize that Canine Companions really and truly expects me to hand over the leash and say goodbye. You're not going to be my puppy any longer. That realization always makes me feel like I've been punched in the stomach."

I stared at her. "What do you mean, I WON'T BE YOUR PUPPY ANY LONGER?" I put my head in her lap and gave her my most doleful look. "Won't you still love me?"

"Of course I will, goofy boy," she said as she rubbed my ears. "What I mean is that you were my puppy, but you're all grown up now, and it's time for you to be someone else's dog." She thought for a minute. "Look, you know how we go to the library, and I take a stack of books home?" I nodded. "But later I take them back, right? I'm just borrowing them from the library; I don't get to keep them. Well, puppy raising is like that. Canine Companions let us borrow you for eighteen months, but now it's time to take you back."

"So you're saying I've hit my due date?" A thought occurred to me: "Hey, you don't always take your books back on time. Maybe you could keep me a little longer."

Marianne laughed and gave me one last pat. "Nope, it doesn't work like that with Canine Companions. It really is time for you to go on to professional training, which I think you will enjoy. But if you decide it isn't for you, that's OK too. We will always love you, no matter what you decide to do." She looked at the clock. "Hey, we really are going to be late for the meeting." She picked up my leash and smiled. "Let's go, puppy of mine. You have a whole lot of people upstairs who want to give you a last hug."

"OK, but let's take that box of tissues with us," I said. "I have a feeling it's going to be a soggy day."

Chow for now! I'm handing over the DogBlog to Ross, but I'll let him know how I'm doing at professional training. Thanks for taking this journey with me.

Love,
Parker

ROSS

HEY, GOOD
LOOKIN'!

R oss was shipped via Continental Airlines on July 23, 2008. I was a little worried that he might be delayed, because it was summer and the airlines (sensibly) have rules about not flying animals in cargo when it's too hot or too cold. However, he avoided the heat by arriving early in the morning.

The Denver puppy raisers are delighted when pups are flown into the Alaska and Continental Airlines cargo terminal at Denver International Airport because of the "puppy room." I don't think that's what it's officially called, but it has a tile floor and a big sink, perfect for a quick bath for a stinky puppy, and for swabbing out a poopy crate there are even paper towels and cleaning supplies.

Ross was only a little stinky, so I gave him a quick buff and fluff and he was good to go. Puppy raiser Elizabeth joined me for the excursion to the airport, and she fed Ross breakfast while I hosed out the shipping crate. He got thoroughly checked out by the pets once we got home, and then he collapsed for a well-deserved nap.

Ross was slated for Canine Companions' breeding program because he was full Lab; I told him if he played his cards right he'd have the best job in the known universe. He had the "Baumann wiggle" and a sweet, gentle personality. He sucked, or as we puppy raisers say, "wubbed" on a giant fleece bone that he'd arrange so it was bent in half. It finally had to be split and sewed into two wubs—"demi-wubs," as John called them. Some intact males can be a handful, but Ross was never obnoxious around the female puppies in training. He was distracted sometimes, especially if one had just come out of or was about to go into heat. (Note: The female puppies in our region all return to Canine Companions intact and are considered candidates for the breeding program. If they are not suitable, for whatever reason, Canine Companions has them spayed and they continue in the program as potential graduate dogs.) We learned to work at the opposite end of the classroom if we wanted Ross to pay attention to us instead of the pretty girl dogs!

Ross was a handsome fellow, with Baumann's extremely large, round head. People often asked if he was mixed with Rottweiler or Mastiff. If Ross were a person, he'd be the popular, easygoing football star in the letter jacket. He was easy to raise, a Steady Eddie kind of dog. He was bomb-proof in public; nothing made him flinch, startle, or otherwise react. We could take him anywhere, confident he'd be a perfect Canine Companions ambassador.

Ross's DogBlog

Smart Puppy

Ross here, new on the blog. Learning the ropes. I'm sure I'll get the hang of it soon—working dogs need more in the brains department than ordinary dogs, so Canine Companions breeds us for brain power. And temperament and health and personality. All of the pups I've met so far have been very cool and very smart—although, admittedly, I've only met a few. I just got here, after all.

Marianne has been working with me on the Canine Companions commands. She's a nice person, but, just between us, I don't think she's a very good instructor. She was trying to teach me something the other night and for the life of me I could not figure out what the heck she wanted. All I knew was that I wasn't getting any cookies, and both of us were pretty frustrated about it.

Mina, one of the keeper dogs, who has been around the block a few times, came into the kitchen and watched for a minute, then looked at Marianne. "I've got this," she said.

"Thank goodness," Marianne sighed.

Mina lay down. Marianne immediately tossed her a treat.

"Hey, how come you got a cookie for doing nothing?"

Mina swallowed. "It wasn't for nothing. Didn't you see me lie down?"

"Yeah. And?"

Mina rolled her eyes. "That's what Marianne wanted! Aren't you listening? And watch what she does with her hand. She's luring you into lying down."

I turned back to Marianne. "Down," she said and moved her hand (with the treat tucked inside) low to the ground away from me.

"Oh, dear Dog," I thought. "Why didn't she just say 'Ross, lie down?'" I fell over.

"YES!" exclaimed Marianne, giving me three treats.

I looked at Mina. "Really? That's it?"

"Yup," she said.

"Ross, down." Marianne moved her hand along the ground in front of me. I flung myself down again. "YES! Good boy!" Marianne gave me two treats.

"Well, this is easy," I said to Mina.

"Ross, down," Marianne said. I obligingly collapsed and got one treat.

"Hey, how come I only got one treat that time?" I had a sinking feeling I wasn't going to like the answer.

Mina scratched her ear. "It's a Canine Companions training thing. When you're first learning a command you get big rewards, many treats. They call it a jackpot. But when Marianne thinks you know the command you get only one treat, or no treats and lots of praise."

"No treats?" I couldn't believe it.

Mina shrugged. "Humans think we work harder if we're not sure if or when the reward is coming."

I heard "Ross, down," and unenthusiastically dropped to the ground.

"Good boy!" Marianne hugged me and ruffled my ears.

"See?" said Mina.

Huh. This was not good. The next time Marianne said down I was ready. I ignored her.

"Ross, don't!" Marianne snapped. "Ross, down."

I looked at Mina. She shook her head. "See, that's the other thing. Once she thinks you know a command, if you don't do it, you get corrected. Then she gives the command again. Honestly? It's best if you just do the command the first time, treat or no treat."

I sighed and lay down.   Marianne picked me up and hugged me. "Mina, thank you for explaining things to Ross."

I squirmed and Marianne set me down. "Listen," I said to her. "In the future can you just tell me what you want? I'm not stupid."

Marianne looked surprised. "What, like 'Ross, when I say shake I want you to give me your paw?'"

"YES!" I exclaimed. "If I had three people cookies I'd give them to you."

Chow for Now!
Ross

REQUIEM FOR A GREYHOUND

There is great sorrow at our house today. Madeleine the Greyhound, assistant puppy raiser and one of my mentors, has gone to the rainbow bridge. I'm sorry that I won't benefit more from her wise counsel during my formative puppy months. Marianne tells me she helped train all five pups before me, plus dozens and dozens of other Canine Companions pups that came to stay at our house over the past seven years.

John wrote a lovely tribute to her last night:

> *Born in April 1997, she was foolishly named "Jazz TomandCathi" (aka"Tom Cat") on her registration papers. She raced once. We don't know what happened, but we believe she may have gotten distracted by something and paused, causing a ten-Greyhound pile-up, or she simply wasn't interested in running after a mechanical bunny. Her short racing career ended, and she was placed with Colorado Greyhound Adoption.*

She came into our lives on March 29, 1999, and was immediately renamed Madeleine J'Ingle McKiernan, in honor of author Madeleine L'Engle. She was a lovely pet, a velveteen dog, a beautiful backyard runner, a careful guardian of the cats in her life, devoted to her stuffed bunny.

She won "Longest Female Greyhound" at the 2001 Colorado Greyhound Adoption picnic (and they didn't even measure her full, lengthy tail, which stayed intact to the end of her life, unusual for Greyhounds).

She was a regular blood donor at the Wheat Ridge Animal Hospital Blood Bank, the area's largest 24-hour veterinary blood bank, until she retired at the mandatory age of eight.

She was an Assistant Puppy Raiser for Canine Companions for Independence, supervising Trevin II, Stryker I, Rolly II, Hudson IV, Parker II, Ross VI, and numerous other Canine Companions pups that came to stay for puppy trades or puppy-sitting.

She was a two-time cancer survivor.

She is now off to run free, rejoining a variety of friends, taking a large part of our hearts with her.

Mine too.

Chow for now.
Ross

HEARTS AND HEROES

I wish I were a little older so I could have gone to the events at the new Canine Companions Miller Family Campus in New York earlier this month. Marianne said I wasn't "reliable" enough for long plane trips yet. I think that's kind of insulting, really; I am housebroken and I can go a good two or three hours between *hurry* breaks now. Surely a plane ride to New York isn't longer than a couple of hours? Anyhow, I was overruled, and since Marianne hides her credit cards I couldn't sneak online and buy my own plane ticket.

I live in the Southwest Region, so when I go to professional training it will be to the campus in Oceanside. But dogs in the Northeast Region will go to school at the new campus in Medford, NY. The old Northeast campus was in a converted pig barn—a functional, but not very spiffy facility—for the past nineteen years. The staff made do as best they could, and many Canine Companions teams graduated over the years.

But the new campus—wow!!

It is BEAUTIFUL and spacious and state of the art; it will enable them to train more dogs and help more people waiting for Canine Companions miracles.

The new campus also has large handicapped-accessible dorm rooms, something that the other regions provide but was lacking at the old Northeast facility. This means that the people who attend the two-week Team Training class (when they are matched with their Canine Companions assistance dog partners) will be able to stay on campus for free in specially designed rooms instead of staying at local hotels. As you can imagine, that will be a huge benefit in so many ways!

Over four hundred people (and who knows how many dogs) attended the grand opening. I hear it was quite a party. Maybe I'll get to attend next year's Hearts and Heroes Gala when I'm more "reliable."

Chow for now!
Ross

SKUNKS AND LADYBUGS AND GIRL SCOUTS — OH MY! GUEST BLOGGER ODEN, HERE ON TRADE

Oden here, filling in this week for Ross, who is with my family in Colorado Springs while I'm in Denver with Marianne and John. One of those way-crazy Canine Companions puppy raiser trades. Dig it.

However, before Ross and I made it home to our traded spaces on Saturday we attended the puppy raiser Halloween party, which is code for "Let's dress the pups in costume for our own amusement." Seriously, what's with humans and clothes? My own fur coat is all I need, thank you very much. But no, I had to wear a PINK PIG COSTUME. I may never fully recover.

Anyhow, some awesome Junior Girl Scouts hosted this shindig. Now, the girls didn't host just because they're really swell kids (which they are). Nope. They are earning their Bronze Award, the highest award a Junior Girl Scout can earn, which they've been working on for the past TWO YEARS. That's like … um … 7 x 2, carry the 1, add 6 ... Well, it's a really long time! For girls who are nine to eleven years old this is a LOT of work.

To earn their Bronze Award they first had to earn several paws full of community service badges. For their final project, they decided to partner with Canine Companions for Independence. Such smart, kind and sensible Girl Scouts! They sewed tiny capes for the stuffed puppies that Canine Companions sells at community events; they helped at the Canine Companions table at the Summerset Festival; they hosted our Halloween party; and they will help with the gift wrapping fundraiser at Borders Books in December.

DOG, these girls have been really busy earning this award. I'm impressed, aren't you? (And a big WOOF WOOF WOOF to their moms and troop leaders, who probably earned some kind of award themselves. Marianne said something about "Celebratory Margaritas," which I think might be a special ceremony for the moms.)

Dig it!
Oden (for Ross)

HAPPILY EVER AFTER

HANG ON TO YOUR COLLARS!

I came back to Denver on Saturday after a lovely week in Colorado Springs with puppy raisers Susan and Dave. After I'd greeted everyone and made sure all my toys were here, I asked Marianne what was new.

WELL!

She got a very serious look on her face and made me sit down next to her. "We got a call from Stu last week," she said.

Stu is the Southwest Regional puppy program manager, so I knew it had to be important news. "What did he say?" I asked anxiously. "Is Parker OK?"

"Parker is fine, but he's being released from the Canine Companions program," Marianne said.

"But WHY?" I yelped in surprise. "I thought we were hopeful about his progress at professional training." I put my head in Marianne's lap. "What went wrong?"

She stroked my head. "We were hopeful, and Parker seemed to be doing pretty well. Nothing 'went wrong,' really, Parker just decided he wasn't interested in being a service dog. His trainer, Seamus, worked very hard with him, but Parker was showing some behaviors that concerned him. For instance, sometimes Parker hid behind Seamus when a stranger approached."

I blinked in surprise. "That doesn't sound like Parker," I said. "Parker was always friendly to everyone when I was with him. Are you sure Stu was calling about the right dog?"

Marianne smiled. "Yes, I'm sure Stu was calling about Parker. Sometimes the dogs show new behaviors in professional training when they are stressed or unhappy. The trainers work with them to determine if the behaviors are only temporary while the dogs adjust to the rigors of the training course, or if it's more serious. Stu said that Seamus worked quite a bit with Parker, and in the end Canine Companions decided that Parker really doesn't want to be an assistance dog."

"Huh," I said. "I didn't know that was an option. Can I decide I don't want to be an assistance dog, too?"

Marianne laughed. "Well, you can, but we hope you don't! It's always up to you, though." She suddenly looked very serious. "You know, Ross, one of the things we like best about Canine Companions is that the trainers always have the safety of the future team in mind, as well as the happiness of the dog. If a dog doesn't like to work, or shows behaviors that might jeopardize his human partner, they know it's best to release the dog from the program. They want to graduate only the dogs that truly love to work and work really well all the time."

"That makes sense. So what happens now? Will Parker come back to live with us?" I asked.

Marianne sighed. "Well, puppy raisers are always asked if they want to take back the puppy they raised. But in our case we don't think Parker will be happy at our house. Since he's no longer a puppy-in-training he can't come to work with John or me, and we don't think he'd like being alone in the house all day with just the kitties and Mina for company."

I nodded. "That's right; he always wanted to be the center of attention and with his humans. So, where will he go?"

"That's the best part!" said Marianne. "Parker will live with our friends Jeannie and Rod here in Denver! He'll have lots of play time with their other dog Nicky and so much attention from Jeannie and Rod." She gave me a hug. "And after he gets settled we can go visit and you can play with him!"

That sounds great to me! So you see, even though Parker isn't graduating as an assistance dog, it's a story with a happy ending. Especially if Jeannie will let him cuddle on the sofa with her.

snickersnickersnicker

Chow for now!
Ross

THE REAL PUPPY RAISERS OF COLORADO

Last night was a quiet evening at home. The cats were snoozing, Mina was nibbling on a chewie bone, John was playing solitaire on the computer, and Marianne was listlessly channel surfing. She paused on a reality TV show featuring a group of women called "The Real Housewives of Atlanta."

We watched for a while in silence.

"Yikes," I finally said. "Those people sure are different from you and your friends. They seem so mean. I think I like your friends better."

"Are you sure?" Marianne teased. "Those women are wealthy; they could buy all the fleece toys, chewies, and dog cookies your heart desires."

I paused for reflection. Unlimited dog cookies? Really? I sighed. "OK, that's tempting, but I still think I prefer puppy raisers. Those Atlanta ladies seem kind of grouchy and they don't have any dogs. I bet that's why they are so unhappy. If they became puppy raisers they'd be much more cheerful."

Marianne smiled. "You might be right. We certainly seem to have a lot more fun, even if we don't have unlimited pots of money. And somehow I think that even if we did have tons of money it would end up supporting Canine Companions causes. Which reminds me, we have that event on Friday night we need to plan."

While Marianne went off to call one of her puppy raiser friends to discuss Friday night's outing, I watched the rest of the show. I decided these are the differences between reality TV and reality:

Real Housewives ...	**Real Puppy Raisers ...**
Have huge, exclusive parties with security guards and bouncers to greet the guests.	Have huge, inclusive parties with a pack of Canine Companions dogs to greet the guests.
Bicker a lot and are mean to each other.	Laugh a lot and do nice things for each other.
Have personal assistants, hairstylists, and makeup artists.	Raise Canine Companions pups to be personal assistants while doing their own hair and makeup, often using that time as a dog training exercise. (Who's afraid of a hair dryer? Not me!)
Decorate their houses with expensive carpets, furniture, and knick-knacks.	Decorate their houses with dog crates, dog toys, and fur.

Shop at Fendi, Prada, and Versace and wear fancy designer dresses.	Shop at Target, PETCO, and PetSmart and wear jeans and Canine Companions shirts.
Compete for the best, fanciest, most expensive, or most exclusive anything.	Share responsibility, joy, and credit.
Spend $20,000 on a kid's birthday party.	Spend about $2,500 raising a Canine Companions puppy.

Real Puppy Raisers think the best news in the world is finding out a pup is graduating. I don't think there's an equivalent for the Real Housewives. Poor things. They don't know what they're missing!

Chow for now!
Ross

LUCKY ME

I heard that this Thursday is a holiday called Thanksgiving.

"What's Thanksgiving? Why is it a holiday? Are dog cookies involved?" I asked Marianne.

"It's all about the cookies with you, isn't it?" she said.

Well—DUH.

"Thanksgiving is a day when we consider our blessings," Marianne said. "For example, I'm thankful for our family and friends, a warm house, plenty of food, and a job I love. I am thankful that we're able to raise Canine Companions puppies like you. And I am thankful that we can have pets as well. I can't imagine life without Mina, Dash, and D'art."

Hmmmm.

"What about the Great Dane you and John applied to adopt?" I asked. "You seem pretty excited about the possibility of another dog in the house, but I'm not quite sure why you seem to think we need one. Aren't Mina and I enough?" I pouted.

"You would think so, but here's the deal: we have room in our house and in our hearts for another dog, and there are so many who need homes. Why not share our good fortune?"

"Oh well, when you put it like that, I guess having another dog to play with would be fun," I said. "In fact, we have room for lots more, don't we? We could adopt ALL of the rescued Great Danes!"

"WHOA, slow down! We have room for ONE more dog. I wish we could adopt them all but our house isn't THAT big!" exclaimed Marianne. "I'm sure they will all find good, loving homes."

Lucky me. I have a warm house, lots and lots of toys and chewie bones, two square meals a day, and, yes, dog cookies. But if you have room in your heart and home, won't you consider adopting an animal? Or if adoption isn't an option, how about making a donation to a shelter or rescue group? I know the animals would be grateful, and so would I. Happy Thanksgiving!

Chow for now!
Ross

LAB CHRISTMAS

I was dozing while Marianne was reading her email and listening to holiday music this morning when I heard some very nice singing. Marianne was smiling and humming along. I sat up to listen.

"What is that?" I asked. "I like it!"

"Me, too," she said. "It's one of my favorite holiday songs, a jazzy version of `White Christmas' recorded by Clyde McPhatter and the Drifters in 1953." She boosted me into her lap and cuddled me to the end of the song.

"I liked the singing and all, but the words weren't very relevant to me," I complained.

"And I suppose you could do better?" Marianne asked, raising one eyebrow.

A challenge! OK, so I'm no Irving Berlin, but I came up with my own version. Sing along if you wish!

Lab Christmas
By Ross

I'm dreaming of a Lab Christmas
When humans grant your every wish.
Where stuffed Kongs glisten,
And puppies listen
To hear kibble in the dish.
I'm dreaming of a Lab Christmas
With every Christmas card I chew.
May your toys be squeaky and soft,
And may all your chewie bones be new.

I'm dreaming of a Lab Christmas
With every ornament I bite.
May your treats be bacon and cheese,
And may all your Christmases delight.

Chow for now and happy holidays!
Ross

SANTA BROUGHT ME A PUPPY!

GUESS WHAT??? SANTA BROUGHT ME A PUPPY FOR CHRISTMAS!

A really BIG puppy!

Meryl is a Great Dane, and she just had her first birthday, so she's five months older than I am. And OK, to be honest, Meryl isn't really *my* puppy; she's part of the family. She's all black, with dabs of white on her chest and paws, and has huge floppy ears.

Santa brought Meryl from a Great Dane rescue group. Sadly, Meryl's first family could no longer keep her, but we are so glad Santa brought her to our house to live! I'm not entirely clear on how Santa got Meryl down the chimney; Santa is pretty crafty. I asked Meryl but she said it was a secret. Rats.

She says she likes our house and big yard and her new GI-NORMOUS crate. Marianne was a little horrified when she realized how big the crate was after it was assembled in the bedroom. She found Meryl and Mina and me sitting in it together! We got a good laugh out of the look on her face.

I'm a little jealous of Meryl at mealtimes. My cup and a half of food looks pretty paltry compared to her four cups! Yeah, yeah, she's ninety pounds to my fifty-five, and Marianne points out that she's really skinny and needs some extra nutrition while she grows into her big self, but still—!

Meryl is a good foot taller than Marianne when she puts her paws on Marianne's shoulders, and I can easily walk under her. My goodness, I had no idea dogs came in this extra-extra large size! But here's the funny part: Mina, all twenty-five pounds of her, is still the boss. When she barks at us we mind our manners. Yes, Ma'am!

Speaking of which, I admit to enjoying watching someone else be the focus of training for a change. Marianne is teaching Meryl manners and some new commands like "No running in the house!" and "No helping yourself to food on the counters!" and "No nibbling!" and "No jumping!" We both hear "No rough-housing inside!" quite often—Marianne thinks the lamps should stay on the tables in one piece.

As usual, the cats have copped an attitude of "Whatever, dude." As long as they still get the majority of lap time they're happy. Funny story: John picked me up yesterday for some Teddy Bear Time (that's what we call it when I get cradled upside down in a lap). Anyhow, I was enjoying the snuggling when Meryl happened upon us. She watched for a minute and then tried to climb into John's lap! He told her that he was sorry, but she's too big for Teddy Bear. He reminded her that she is allowed on the bed and can get her special snuggle time that way.

I hope your holiday was as excellent as mine, and I wish you joy, lots of cookies, and long naps in the New Year.

Chow for Now!
Ross

LAUNDRY MUTT

Last Sunday evening we were relaxing when I suddenly smelled something funny. Marianne looked at me and said "Do you smell something burning?" (For a human, she has a pretty good nose.) We rushed in to the kitchen and turned off the dryer. John and Marianne pulled it away from the wall and cleaned out all the lint (which I offered to eat) from the hoses. But when Marianne turned it on again, the burning smell came back. So, no more dryer until a repairman can look at it.

"But what about my cape?" I fretted. "My cape still needs to be washed, doesn't it?"

"You are such a worrywart," Marianne sighed. "First of all, I already washed and dried your cape, so it's nice and clean. Second, I can hand wash it or even wash it in the dishwasher in a pinch. And third, we'll just take our clothes to a Laundromat until the dryer is fixed."

"A laundro-what?" I asked.

"A Laundromat is a business with washers and dryers. I'll take you with me so you can see it," Marianne promised.

So, this week Marianne loaded up all the clothes, sheets, and towels, and we drove over to a Laundromat. We picked an empty row of washers and Marianne started putting clothes into them. "You know, you might have to help someone do laundry someday," she remarked.

I watched for a few minutes. "How could I help?"

"Well, you could put items into a laundry basket, carry or drag the basket into the laundry room or Laundromat, and take items out of the basket and drop them into the washer or dryer," she explained. "If you end up working as a Hearing Dog you could alert your partner to the buzzer when the washer is out of balance or when the dryer is finished with its cycle."

"But I don't know how to do those things and I never have understood the whole sorting thing you do! What if I goof and put a dog toy in with the sheets or something?" I worried.

"You don't have to know how to sort the laundry; your partner will tell you what goes where, and the trainers at professional training will teach you how to do the rest. For example, they might put a rope on the laundry basket and teach you how to pull it. And rest assured, putting a dog toy in with the sheets would not be a fatal mistake."

Oh. OK. I relaxed a little bit and watched as Marianne finished sorting the clothes and carefully sprinkled soap in the machines.

"Now I need to feed the washers," she said, rummaging around in her purse.

FOOD? I perked up. "Does Eukanuba make washer kibble? Can I have some?"

"No, you silly boy, I meant I need to put quarters into the machines. Sorry, I didn't mean to get your hopes up." She put quarters into the machines, which began making sloshing sounds.

Just then the door opened and a sleepy-looking fellow shambled in, dragging a large plastic garbage bag. He stopped in front of a big washer and shoved the contents of the bag into it, dumped soap on top, and slammed the lid. After starting the machine, he picked up the empty bag and shambled back out.

"Wow," I said. "That didn't take long. How come he just put everything in one machine?"

"That," Marianne said, "is what I call Guy Laundry. Shove everything into one machine, no sorting and no regard for color or type of item or fabric. Works fine if you don't care if everything is a uniform shade of dingy."

Soon our clothes were ready to go into the dryers. Marianne sorted things again into piles in a wheeled cart and then put each pile into a separate dryer. "How do you know which pile each item goes into?" I asked.

"Well, these things are delicate so they only go in the dryer for ten minutes on low heat. These towels are heavy and will take longer, so I'll put them in another dryer for twenty minutes on high heat," she explained, feeding more quarters into the dryers.

"Will I have to learn how to put the quarters in, too?"

"Probably not, but you might have to pick up a quarter off the floor if your partner dropped it. You'll learn how to pick up all kinds of things at professional training."

I was pondering this when the sleepy guy came in and put everything from the washer into one of the wheeled carts. He took it over to a dryer, shoved everything into it, put in three quarters, turned it on high, and sat in a chair to wait.

"More Guy Laundry?" I said.

"Yup, and watch what happens when it's done," Marianne advised.

While she finished sorting and folding our laundry, the sleepy guy's dryer stopped. He walked over with the plastic bag and carelessly stuffed all of the clothes from the dryer into the bag. He shambled back out.

"Won't those things be kind of wrinkled?" I asked. "And he didn't really seem to check to see if everything was dry, so won't some things still be damp?"

"Yes, that's Guy Laundry." Marianne gave me a hug. "You're such a smart puppy, and you will be a big help to your partner some day."

I hope I'm up to the challenge, but I have to admit, Guy Laundry looks a whole lot easier!

Chow for now!
Ross

TICKING CLOCK

Tuesday afternoon seemed very ordinary. While Marianne unpacked groceries, Mina, Meryl and I had a good romp in the backyard. We came in and were settling in for a nice sunny nap in the den when we heard a shriek from the kitchen. What on earth?

All three of us raced to the kitchen to find Marianne standing in the middle of the room with a very shocked look on her face. She held a letter in her hand, which shook slightly. "What is it?" we clamored. "Are you OK? What happened? Is it bad news?" Meryl leaned over and gave Marianne a big slurpy kiss, which seemed to revive her a bit.

"Oh, Ross," she said sadly. "It's a letter from Canine Companions about your turn-in date."

"Is that all?" Mina snorted. She and Meryl went back into the den.

I cocked my head and said, "November, right? That's when I go to professional training, November, when I'll be eighteen months old." I wagged my tail.

"Um, yes, that's when we thought it would be." Marianne paused and took a deep breath. "But this letter is the official notification. Your turn-in date is August 22."

I yelped in surprise. "But that's just barely a year after you got me!" I protested. "I'm not sure I'll be ready to go to professional training in August! Heck, I'm still in the Basic puppy class. I have a lot to learn! Why would Canine Companions change the date?"

Marianne sighed. "It's complicated, Ross. Canine Companions has to carefully balance the number of dogs already in professional training with the number of dogs slated to turn in, and then factor in the number of people on the waiting list and the kinds of dogs needed. It's possible that there were more dogs released from the program than expected, or more dogs chosen as breeders. Yes, it's three months earlier than we expected, and certainly sooner than we'd like. But the bottom line is that you're Canine Companions' dog and they decide when you're ready for professional training." She looked at me sternly. "That means you need to stop being such a teenager and start working a little harder so you will be ready for professional training in August."

I groaned, but she had a point. I guess the next six months are going to be pretty intense. No more pretending I don't know what a command means, no more expecting treats for good behavior, no more faking deafness when "Ross, here!" is called, no more acting like *stay* is more of a theory than an actual command. Rats.

Marianne gave me a hug and a shaky smile. "Oh, cheer up! The clock is ticking, but we still have six months together. Come on, let's get a few treats and work on some of your commands."

At least I don't have to give up treats yet.

Chow for now!
Ross

EXILE!

"Banished!" I moaned. "Exiled! Cast out, deported, dismissed, ostracized, ousted!"

"Are you done?" Marianne inquired drily.

I thought. "Outlawed. Relegated. Shut out."

Marianne rolled her eyes. "Ross, you are none of those things. You're simply going to stay with other puppy raisers for a week, that's all."

"But why?" I whined. "Don't you love me? I thought you LOVED me."

"When you're like this, maybe not so much," she grumbled. But then she ruffled my ears and relented. "Look, the reason we need you to spend some time away is that Meryl is going to have surgery and she'll need to be quiet for a week so she can recover. That means no jumping, galloping, roughhousing, or playing chase with you. It will be easier on her if you're not around to tempt her into a wrestling match."

"What kind of surgery? Is she going to be OK?" Now I was worried.

"She'll be fine. It's a procedure called gastropexy. The vet will make a tiny incision and tack Meryl's stomach to the wall of her abdomen so it will never twist."

"Oh," I said. "But why would her stomach twist?"

"Some breeds of dogs are prone to something called 'bloat' where the stomach becomes too full of air," Marianne explained. "When this happens the stomach can twist, and both the inlet and the outlet of the stomach become twisted shut. It's lethal if not corrected really fast. Our vet is familiar with Great Danes and recommended that Meryl have the surgery."

"Oh, I like Dr. Vicksman! He gives me cookies," I said. "OK, if Dr. V. says this will be good for Meryl then I'll go stay with another puppy raiser family. But they better have toys and cookies!"

Chow for now!
Ross

Tashi the Terrific

Did you know that some Canine Companions dogs graduate as Hearing Dogs? I was curious about that kind of job, so I contacted Hearing Dog Tashi to get the full story. She and her partner Stan live in New Mexico.

ROSS: Where did you grow up? And where did you go to professional training?

TASHI: I grew up in Sammamish, Washington. I went to professional training at the Northwest Region in Santa Rosa, California. That is also the National Headquarters for Canine Companions and the only region that trains Hearing Dogs. During my initial professional training the trainers noticed that I had some traits that they thought would make me a good candidate for a Hearing Dog.

ROSS: Like what?

TASHI: I'm very curious about sounds that I haven't heard before. I'm not afraid of them, and I can locate them quickly with just my ears even if I can't see what is making the noise. So, Canine Companions put me in the Hearing Dog program.

ROSS: What was the training like?

TASHI: My trainer, Ken, taught me how to alert someone when I hear one of the "special" sounds, like a telephone, doorbell, alarm clock, or smoke detector.

ROSS: How did you get matched with Stan?

TASHI: I actually went through TWO Team Trainings. I wasn't the best match with any of the people in my first Team Training, so Ken kept practicing with me, and then a couple months or so later there was another Team Training.

ROSS: And was that when you matched with Stan?

TASHI: YES! Stan was at the second Team Training. I fell in love with Stan right away. Ken must have noticed it since he matched Stan and me.

Team Training was a lot of fun, especially since it's the *people* that have to learn everything! The trainers at Canine Companions have already taught us dogs what we need to know before Team Training starts. Ken taught Stan how to introduce me to new sounds, and Stan and I practiced the sounds that Ken had taught me, along with all of the other things we needed to know to work together. Practicing sounds means treats, so I got a lot of them from Stan.

ROSS: Hey, that sounds like training I'd enjoy. Yum, treats ... Oh, sorry, I got distracted there for a minute. What kind of jobs do you do for Stan?

TASHI: I wake Stan up every morning when his alarm goes off. I tell him when I hear the phone ring at home, I let him know if someone knocks on the door of his office at work, and I have a timer that I tell him about when I hear it. My favorite of all the commands and sounds is *Go get Stan!*

ROSS: Wait, you mean you retrieve Stan?   That's funny!

TASHI: Right! If Becky, Stan's wife, is in another part of the house and wants Stan for something, she calls me. When I get to her she tells me *Go get Stan!* and I get to run through the house back to where Stan is and alert him and take him to Becky. That also works at church if someone wants to talk to Stan.

ROSS: How do you alert Stan?

TASHI: Good question! I nudge him in the leg with my nose. If I can't reach his leg for some reason, I'll nudge him in the side, like in the morning when I wake him up, or if he's lying on the couch watching TV. Once I've nudged him enough to get his attention, he'll look at me and tell me "Yes." I know that I can stop nudging when he does that because a treat always follows the word "yes."

ROSS: Clearly this is something I need to train Marianne to do! She doesn't hand out nearly enough treats.

TASHI: Then Stan will ask me "What?" and I take him to the sound I've heard. When I get to the sound I might touch it with my nose or point to it with my nose when I'm close to it. Stan tells me that magic word "Yes!" again, and I get another treat. So working for Stan is a lot of fun.

ROSS: Are you learning new things?

TASHI: Yes! Just last week I started learning the sound of Stan's carbon monoxide detector and the smoke detector. You know, all the different brands of electronic gadgets make different noises. The smoke detector or phone at Canine Companions might not sound like the ones at Stan's house, so I have to learn new sounds all the time.

ROSS: Boy, you working dogs really do work a LOT, don't you? What do you like to do for fun?

TASHI: My favorite thing is play time in the yard. I like to run as fast as my legs will move. My puppy raisers and Stan call this "zoom-butt."

ROSS: *snickersnickersnicker* Yeah, I love that too! The puppy raisers in Denver call it Cracker Dog. What else should I know about you and Stan?

TASHI: I love getting belly rubs from Stan. Stan thinks it's funny when I'm curled up on my mat or bed in his office or at home and I snore without even closing my eyes. Oh, and meeting new people is always fun, too. Especially the people that see Stan and me out someplace and say "AWW!" I can't help it, it makes my tail wag.

ROSS: Yes, that "AWW!" is the best, isn't it?

Chow for now!
Ross

You Know You're a Puppy Raiser When ...

The other night the puppy raisers were entertaining themselves with a little game they call "You Know You're a Puppy Raiser When ..." They seemed to find it hugely amusing, though I can't say I really understood why. I mean, aren't they describing pretty much everyone? Marianne assured me that, no, puppy raisers are a group unto themselves, but other humans who love dogs would probably find it funny and familiar too. Huh. I'll let you be the judge.

For your amusement, then, I present (with thanks to puppy raisers everywhere for contributing) You Know You're a Puppy Raiser When...

- You have crates, collars, and Gentle Leaders in every size, style, and color.
- You accept dog hair as an accessory AND a condiment.
- Dog crates double as end tables.
- You have more dog towels than people towels in your house (and your spouse knows the difference).
- You purchase a car based on how many dogs and/or crates it will carry.

- Your co-workers know all the Canine Companions commands, and there's a chorus of "DON'T!" when the puppy dives for a tidbit on the floor.

- You have photos of your puppy on your desk, but none of your spouse or kids (unless they happen to be in the puppy photo).

- The various snacks you keep at your desk consist of chicken, liver, and beef flavors.

- The contents of your purse, backpack, or briefcase includes hand sanitizer, poop bags, a chewie bone, dog cookies, a water bottle, and a collapsible dish.

- You automatically *wait* at doorways, even when the dog isn't with you.

- You attend an event because it's a good training opportunity for the puppy, not because you have any real interest in the activity.

- You can scoop poop in public without embarrassment while maintaining a conversation about Canine Companions.

- At a restaurant you can simultaneously carry on a conversation with your dinner companions and monitor your puppy's behavior under the table.

- You watch *Animal Planet* because the puppy enjoys it.

- People don't recognize you without the puppy and/or they know the pup's name but not yours.

- You're overheard telling your kids "Drop it!" or "Leave it!" or snapping "Don't!" in your best puppy raiser correction voice.

- You look for a parking place near a good *hurry* spot, rather than near the store.

- Every pocket of every jacket, vest, and sweatshirt has dog cookies in it. While folding laundry, you've found dog cookies (intact) in the pockets of your jeans.

- Your four-year-old can deliver a near-perfect Canine Companions spiel, knows the proper use of all the commands, and can take over for you in puppy class.

- You've burst into tears listening to a sad song on the radio because it reminds you that turn-in is approaching.

- And last but not least, you know you're a puppy raiser when your greatest joy in life is handing over your dog's leash to a perfect stranger at a Canine Companions Graduation.

Chow for now!
Ross

ARE YOU SURE THAT'S A CAT?

Life is just full of surprises, isn't it? Like the giant snowstorm yesterday. Really, one minute it was warm and sunny and the next POW! Tons of snow to romp around in.

But that's not the biggest surprise this week. As we were driving home from work yesterday, John said, "There's a little surprise waiting for us at the house, Ross."

"Really? What kind of surprise? A new toy?   FOOD?" I wagged my tail hopefully.

But John wouldn't say any more, except to admonish me that the surprise was certainly NOT a toy or food, but it was a good surprise. I couldn't imagine what that would be if it wasn't a toy or food. I kind of hoped it wasn't another Great Dane. Meryl's plenty.

We walked into the house, and I immediately began to hunt for the surprise. It wasn't hard to find, since Mina was lying outside the guest room door, peering underneath and whining. Much to my surprise, a long, skinny, fuzzy orange paw snaked under the door, waved at us, and retreated.

I jumped. "What was that?!"

Mina replied, "That's our new kitty. Marianne brought him home today. I am SO excited to meet him! But Marianne says we have to be patient and let him settle in first."

Just then we heard the rattle of our food dishes so we left the kitty and ran out to the kitchen. Fun's fun, but dinner only happens once a day. (Why is that, I wonder?) Anyhow, after I ate I asked Marianne how we came to acquire another cat.

"Well, since D'Artagnan died last month the house feels a little empty."

I nodded. I was too sad to blog about it at the time, but I should explain that we recently lost D'Art, our elder statescat. He was nineteen and had been suffering from what Marianne called "the dwindles." Nothing traumatic, no terrible illness, just a slow extinguishing of his life light. He has been sorely missed.

Marianne rubbed my ears. "I thought Dash was especially missing having a kitty pal. So I've been checking shelters online. When I saw the photo of Louie I knew I had to go meet him and see if he was a fit for our family. He said he'd like to come live with us, even after I told him about Meryl, so here he is."

I stared at the door to the guest room. "How did you know he was the right kitty for our family?"

"There were several nice kitties there, but Louie is the one who caught my eye. He's so dear and funny looking!" Marianne sighed happily. "I had to fill out an application and be approved, which was kind of nerve-wracking. Luckily the shelter decided we were a good fit for Louie and I was able to bring him home this afternoon. Just wait 'til you see him!"

Hmmmm. I admit that the paw I saw did look different than Dash's paw, but all cats look pretty much alike, don't they? Marianne said I'd have to wait and see. She explained that cats a need a longer adjustment period in a new home than dogs do. So we're meeting him one at a time, and he's hanging out in the guest room until he's completely comfortable. He and Dash are already fast friends, so Dash hangs out with him sometimes. But I guess the dogs are too big and noisy for him all at once.

I got my chance to meet him this morning. Marianne invited me into the guest room where she was drinking her coffee and reading the paper. I looked around for Louie.

Marianne pointed. "Don't you see him? He's lying under the covers. See his head?"

I blinked. "You said he was a cat. That's not a cat—he doesn't look anything like D'Art or Dash. He looks like one of the goblins from Gringotts Bank!" (We're fond of Harry Potter around here.) I sniffed. "He smells like a cat," I admitted, "but he's weird looking, with those huge eyes and giant bat ears."

Louie snaked out from under the covers and glared at me. "Who're you calling funny looking?" he demanded. I inched closer and sniffed again. Louie gave a low growl and smacked my nose.

"HEY!" I yelped, blinking back tears. "That hurt!"

"Ross, back up and give him space," Marianne admonished. "I told you he needs time. Take it easy." Louie gave me a smug look and crawled back under the covers. I heard a very loud rumbling noise.

"What on earth is that noise? Is that the cat?"

Marianne laughed. "Yes, he has a very loud purr, doesn't he?"

I'll say. The windows were rattling! Dash has a very tiny purr, very hard to hear unless he's lying on your ear. This cat sounded like a race car.

I curled up on the floor and warily watched the mound under the covers. "What kind of cat is he? He's different than anything I've seen before."

"Louie is an Oriental Shorthair. His small triangular head, large almond eyes, and big ears are part of the breed standard. And Orientals come in almost any color, including Louie's orange marmalade," explained Marianne. "I looked the breed up on the Cat Fanciers web site."

"Are you going to call him Louie?" I asked. "I thought you and John named all the cats with 'D' names, like D'Art and Dash."

"And Dogberry, Dylan, Drizzle, and Dhurrie," she agreed. "Yes, we're trying to think of another name. Louie is what they were calling him at the shelter. I'm leaning toward Dewey Decibel for his loud purr. What do you think we should call him?"

"Diablo," I suggested, rubbing my nose and wincing. "Demon. Dervish."

Marianne rolled her eyes. "Oh, stop being such a baby. He didn't hurt anything but your pride. Give him a few more days and you'll be good pals."

Chow for now!
Ross

REPRIEVE!

Marianne was checking her email when she suddenly gave a yelp, leaped up, and did a little dance around the room. I jumped to my feet and wagged my tail.

"What's up?" I asked.

"You have a reprieve, a reprieve, a reprieve!" she sang joyously.

"I'm so happy! I have to call John right away!" She picked up the phone and reported this happy news to John. When she hung up she sat back down and began furiously typing. "I need to tell Pat and Vanessa and Elizabeth and Diane and Jessica and Jennifer."

"Excellent!" I watched her. "Um, can I ask a question?"

"Sure," said Marianne as she kept typing.

"What's a reprieve?"

She looked at me. "Oh, I'm sorry, Ross! I should have explained. A reprieve usually means a respite from impending punishment or a death sentence ..."

"A DEATH SENTENCE? WHAT!?!"

"Let me finish!" Marianne laughed, pulling me over for a hug. "In this case reprieve means a postponement of your turn-in date. You don't have to go to professional training until November after all!"

Oh.

OH!!

"That is good news! Whew! Now I can slack off a bit and not work so hard; what a relief! I was really stressing about learning all those advanced commands by August."

Marianne gave me a stern look. "You don't have to stress about learning your commands, but you don't get to slack off, Buster. I still expect you to pay attention in class and keep working on the advanced commands."

When she calls me "Buster" I know she means business. So, the good news is I get to stay with my puppy raisers for three more months. The bad news is that I have to work just as hard. Shoot.

Chow for now!
Ross

ADVENTURES IN SNOWMASS

A few weeks ago I got to do something really cool. I attended the National Disabled Veterans Winter Sports Clinic in Snowmass Village with a puppy raiser named Pat. Pat attends every year so she can talk to the veterans about Canine Companions dogs. This year Pat invited me to go along with her, because her current puppy, Hyde, was too little. Hyde had a fabulous time at my house and was spoiled outrageously by my co-workers at 7News who declared him the Cutest Puppy Ever. Huh—I remember when I held that title. Such fickle, fickle people.

Anyhow, this was the twenty-third time this event has been held, and this year there were over four hundred participants. The clinic is sponsored by the Department of Veterans Affairs and Disabled American Veterans for veterans with disabilities including spinal cord injuries, amputations, visual impairment, and brain injuries. The veterans learn adaptive skiing and also get to try other adaptive sports, including scuba diving, sled hockey, snowshoeing, snowmobiling, rock climbing, trap shooting, fencing, and golf. There are snowcat & gondola rides, a trip to the hot springs, and workshops on all kinds of topics.

That's where Pat and I came in. We did an evening presentation on Canine Companions with some friends. Pat talked about puppy raising and how Canine Companions dogs go from eight-week-old balls of fluff to working dogs. Her friend, Buddy, is a veteran and graduated with Canine Companions dog Ellie a few years ago. Buddy told the veterans all about Ellie and all the cool things she does to help Buddy be independent. Another puppy raiser, JoAnn, described the Hearing Dog program. The audience was very interested and asked lots of great questions. Pat said one veteran was so inspired that he opened his laptop and filled out the online Canine Companions application during the presentation!

During the day, Pat and I watched some of the activities. There are more than two hundred certified ski instructors for the disabled, including several current and former members of the U.S. Disabled Ski Team, who volunteer as ski instructors. There was even a race training and development program to help veterans develop their skiing abilities to an elite level, with the ultimate goal of qualifying for the U.S. Paralympics Team. The vets are amazing as they learn how to use the adaptive equipment and are soon flying down the mountain on different types of skis, many of them for the very first time. I wanted to try out the monoski, but Pat said no. Darn.

We went to the large dining area each night, just to visit with the vets and their families and answer questions about Canine Companions. Pat told Marianne that she let me "get all the hugs, kisses, and 'wonderful handsome dog' comments he could handle." Needless to say, that was my favorite part!

The week flew by and was over too soon. Next year, Hyde will be old enough to go with Pat, and I'll be at professional training. Maybe, just maybe, I'll graduate with a veteran! How cool would that be?

Chow for now!
Ross

TOMMY TIME

Oh my stars and collars, I have incredibly exciting news!

My friend Tommy, who was raised here in Denver by Vanessa and Kevin, is graduating as a Facility Dog this weekend! Marianne is going to Oceanside to cheer him on, though I have to stay home because she's taking a pup named Griffin—who was raised at Kit Carson Correctional Center—for turn-in. That's another story.

ANYHOW, I called right away to get all the details about Tommy, and Kevin was happy to oblige.

ROSS: Was Tommy a pretty easy puppy?

KEVIN: Tommy was a very easy puppy, but he had nonstandard puppy issues.

ROSS: How so?

KEVIN: It started from the moment we met him. Tommy's sister Tambia was raised by Mitzi and Klif in Golden, Colorado. When we went to pick up Tommy at DIA's Cargo terminal, we knew that Tambia and Tommy were on the same flight. Well, when they brought the crates forward, one puppy was less than pleased about the day's events, and the other pup was quiet. It turned out that the upset puppy was Tambia, and the quiet puppy was Tommy. We were a bit relieved at that moment, but it was a foreshadowing of Tommy's personality. He never barked and was very easy in public (no whining), but he was a very deliberate dog. Tommy helped teach us patience, as our world now operated on "Tommy Time."

ROSS: Hmmmm, Marianne has told me once or twice that I'm on Tommy Time. What does it mean?

KEVIN: My best Tommy Time story is the contrast of Tommy and Tambia at a Cherry Creek Mall puppy class. We walked from the middle of the mall to Nordstrom. It took Tommy and me close to twenty minutes to walk that short distance. Other handlers were jokingly asking us if we decided to go do a little side shopping excursion. On the way back, I walked with Tambia. We covered that same distance in about four minutes. Tambia and Tommy couldn't be more different.

ROSS: Right, Tommy Time.

KEVIN: And then there's his appearance. Tommy is one-quarter Golden Retriever and three-quarters Labrador. At least that's what Canine Companions told us. I think he is half lap dog and half Muppet. He doesn't look or stand like most Canine Companions dogs, but he is about the most snuggly, lovable dog I have ever come across.

ROSS: Half Muppet?

KEVIN: Tommy has a long body, but with fairly short legs. His black coat looks Lab-like, except with longer fur on his tail and around his chest and neck. He kind of looked like a lion with a ruff. As much as we watched his diet, he didn't have the usual Canine Companions taper at the hips. As you know, a big no-no is turning back a portly dog to Canine Companions for professional training. We tried our best, but nature had its own ideas, so he always looked a little pudgy. He has long ears relative to the rest of his body and he has sad, down-turned eyes. When he sat, his front feet would turn out like a ballerina and he tended to roll to one hip.

ROSS: Did you think Tommy would graduate?

KEVIN: A puppy raiser is always hopeful. We knew he didn't have the energy level of a Hearing Dog. He seemed to like to work bankers' hours (no offense to bankers), so this narrowed the scope. Tommy was incredibly easy to work with in public. Nothing ever seemed to bother him. He also loved to nuzzle up to people in general, and children in particular, so I thought he would be a great Skilled Companion or Facility Dog.

ROSS: Tell me about his match!

KEVIN: Tommy will be a Facility Dog at the Comprehensive Combat and Complex Casualty Care facility at the Navy Medical Center San Diego. Tommy is their first Facility Dog! He'll have three handlers (all physical therapists and/or occupational therapists), but one primary handler. He'll go home with his primary handler at night and spend his days helping the patients, many of whom are amputees. Stu said that when they saw what a "unique temperament" Tommy had, the trainers knew he was the dog for the job.

ROSS: Sounds like a good match for Tommy.

KEVIN: It's not just good, it's perfect! One of the many great aspects of Canine Companions is that they seem to know what is best for the dogs and put them in a position to succeed. When we found out that Tommy was going to be working with men and women who have suffered significant injuries, it made complete sense. While some might consider Tommy's deliberate nature a hindrance to a successful working career, Canine Companions saw the opportunity to place him in an environment where he can help a person learn how to walk with a prosthetic limb. Tommy's steady, unflappable, and lovable nature is the perfect complement to the skills of the physical and occupational therapists working with our soldiers. Can you tell we are very proud of Tommy and feel very fortunate that he will be working with such special people?

ROSS (wagging tail): Yeah, I think that's pretty wonderful myself. What's your secret to raising a successful Facility Dog?

KEVIN: I think the secret is within the dog. I believe it's eighty to ninety percent whether the dog wants to be an assistance dog, and the balance is the puppy raising village helping with the socialization and training. So Ross, it's up to you!

ROSS: Yup, and I'm not telling what my plans are just yet. Any final thoughts?

KEVIN: We love all of the Canine Companions dogs that have come through our house. We love all of the people we've met through the Canine Companions organization, specifically, and the people we have met at various public activities. I am certainly proud that Canine Companions has identified an opportunity to reach out and work with our servicemen and women who have sacrificed for this country. I can't think of a better partnership than Canine Companions' skilled staff with our soldiers. Vanessa and I are proud to be a small cog in this linkage.

ROSS: Shoot, now you made me cry.

Chow for now!
Ross

TRAVEL DOG

Imagine my surprise last week when Marianne loaded me into the car after work WITHOUT DINNER.

"HEY!" I protested, "You forgot to feed me!"

"No, we didn't," said Marianne. "You're going on a trip with John, and we don't think it would be a good idea for you to eat before you get on the plane."

"But WHY?" I whined.

Marianne sighed. "Look, Ross, there's no place for you to *hurry* on the airplane. It's better if your system is empty to prevent any embarrassing accidents, OK? You'll just have to trust us on this."

"Ross, I promise to feed you the minute we land," said John.

HARRUMPH. No food makes me grumpy.

We arrived at the airport along with half the population of Denver, or so it seemed. After checking in we walked over to a long line.

"What's this for?" I asked.

"This is the security line," said John. "Now pay attention. When we get to the front of the line I'm going to take off your collar and leash, which will go through the X-ray machine with my shoes and carry-on bag. When it's our turn to go through the metal detector I'm going to tell you *sit-stay*. I will walk through the arch and then call you. I want you to walk directly to me and sit in front of me. Can you do that?"

I rolled my eyes. 'Yes, I can do that. What do you take me for, a five-month-old puppy?' I was still feeling annoyed about missing dinner.

John patted my head. "I'm sorry about your dinner, but try not to dwell on it. I'll give you your fleece bone once we settle on the plane."

When we got to the front of the line, John grabbed a gray plastic bin and put his jacket, cell phone, and carry-on bag in it. Then he took off his shoes. Then he took off his belt. Then he emptied his pockets.

"Jeez, no wonder this line took so long!" I said.

"Yes, well, nothing we can do about it," John said as he removed my collar and leash. "SIT," he said firmly, and I did. The fellow by the arch motioned for John to walk forward. I heard several people say "Wow, look at that good dog," which made me feel proud. I sat a little straighter. Then John said "Ross, HERE!" and I walked very quickly through the arch and sat in front of him. "Good boy!" John said as he put my collar back on. The security people patted my head and said I did really well. I smiled at them.

As we walked to the gate I asked, "Where are we going anyhow? And why isn't Marianne coming with us?"

"We're going to Indianapolis to visit my sister Linda, her husband Ron, and their kids," said John. "Their youngest, Sabbath, is graduating from high school this weekend, and it's Linda's birthday. Marianne is staying home to care for the pets."

Ah.

Several people came over to admire me and ask John questions about Canine Companions while we were waiting to board the plane. This happens all the time, but John and Marianne never seem to get tired of talking about me and Canine Companions.

Finally we walked into the plane. John stepped into a row of seats and sat down in the one by the window. He said, "Ross, UNDER," and pointed to the tiny space under the seat.

"What? You must be joking," I said. "Look, there's an empty seat next to you. I'll sit there."

I started to climb into the seat, but John shook his head. "NO. You don't get to sit on the furniture at home, and it's the same here. You need to lie down under the seat. Go on, you'll see, it will be fine."

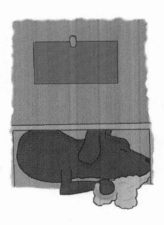

With a little effort I managed to curl up under the seat. John gave me my fleece bone, and I drifted off to sleep. I slept most of the flight, but woke up when we landed. John told me to be patient just a little longer. I EVENTUALLY got my dinner while we waited for his checked bag. We waited in another line to get our rental car. "Don't shed," joked John as we got in. HA HA. Human humor.

It was late when we finally crawled into bed, which turned out to be an air mattress on the floor. I was amused that John had to sleep on the floor, but he didn't seem to mind at all. I curled up next to him. Air mattresses are squishy.

On Sunday we went to Sabbath's graduation ceremony and sat close to the LOUD band. Afterwards we mingled with the graduates and their families. I posed for pictures with Sabbath and her friends. I could tell they thought I was cute and I got lots of hugs.

On Monday John told me we were off on my first camping adventure. We hiked through some beautiful woods in Clifty Falls State Park. Back at our campsite, John set up a flexible crate and a bed for me just before a big rain storm came. We sat under a nearby picnic shelter while it rained. When it was time for bed, I got in the crate like usual, but, to my astonishment, John crawled in behind me.

"What are you doing in my crate?" I exclaimed.

John burst out laughing. "Ross, this isn't a crate, it's a tent. When humans go camping we sleep in tents. And look, this isn't a dog bed, it's a sleeping bag." John unzipped one side and lay down. He zipped it back up, and I curled up next to him and listened to the night noises as we drifted off to sleep. I decided I liked camping.

Then, after one more day with the family back in Indianapolis, it was time to fly home. This time I knew what to expect, including no dinner and the tiny space under the seat. *sigh* But when we landed and walked outside, Marianne was waiting for us. I was excited to see her and tell her all about our trip.

Chow for now!
Ross

PUPARAZZI

At last, the recognition I deserve. The Puparazzi came to my house on Saturday and it was wonderful!

Haley Poulos and her colleague Greg are professional photographers. They showed up at our house early Saturday morning with cameras, lenses, and even a giant reflector to bring out my cheekbones. Bet you didn't know Labradors had cheekbones, did you?

They took about a million photos of me. They took a few of Meryl and Dash and Mina and Dewey and even Marianne, but I was the focal point. I mean, all you have to do is look at the photos on Haley's website to know that Labs are her favorite creatures on Earth. Yeah, OK, there are a few photos of horses and chickens, but clearly she loves Labs best.

I asked Meryl to play with me in the backyard so they could get lots of great action shots of ears and tails and flying feet. I showed Meryl how to pose by pretending to be interested in the leaf Greg was holding up. "Look at the leaf, yummy leaf, beautiful leaf!"

Mina got brave enough to venture outside for a few photos, but every time Greg would stand up she'd bark her fool head off and slink around the yard like some kind of wild African dog. She's a little shy with new people, even when all they want to do is take her picture.

After an hour or so of outdoor photos, we went inside. Meryl and I gulped down a bowl of water and cooled off while Dash the cat monopolized Haley and Greg. Truthfully, I was a little embarrassed for Dash. I think he has secretly been watching *America's Next Top Model*, because he was "working it" as they say. Draping himself on the coffee table, posing on the piano, opening his eyes, closing his eyes, smiling mysteriously, turning his head this way and that. Shameless.

Dewey, on the other hand, mostly sat in the rocking chair and watched, allowing his photo to be taken but not posing as flagrantly as Dash. When Meryl wandered over and prodded him with her nose he leaped to his feet and turned into Ninja Kitty. "HI-YA!" he growled and whacked Meryl on her nose. Meryl blinked and took a step back.

"Hey now," said Greg anxiously.

"It's OK," I told him. "They do this all the time. It's a game called Grouchy Kitty, Laughing Great Dane."

"That's right, big chicken dog," Dewey snarled. "Back off, or I'll turn you into Great Dane on Toast." He hissed ferociously. In the interest of family harmony, Meryl decided it was time for a nap in another room.

After Haley and Greg left, I asked Marianne when we could see the photos. "I think we'll see them on Monday," she promised.

Sure enough, Marianne called me over to the computer this morning to look at Haley's blog. "Look, Ross! Our photos are up. Aren't they great?"

I studied the photos as she scrolled through them. "That's odd," I said. "There seem to be more of Meryl and Mina and the cats than me."

Marianne nodded. "Well, yeah, they took lots of photos of all of us. This was a present for John after all, and he wanted photos of everyone."

I frowned. "But I thought ... well, I assumed ... um ... ," I hesitated.

"Oh poor baby, you thought they were here to just take photos of you, didn't you?" Marianne sighed. "I swear, you Canine Companions dogs think the world revolves around you, and you alone."

"I don't think I take your meaning," I said. "We are SPECIAL dogs, after all. I thought these photos were for the Canine Companions calendar or a newsletter or public relations brochures."

"Perhaps that will happen some day," Marianne said, rubbing my ears just the way I like. "But for now, these photos are a present for John."

I leaned into her for more ear rubbing and sighed blissfully. "Fine, but let's get lots of prints for my Canine Companions baby book, OK?"

Chow for now!
Ross

In Memory of Ivar

This has not been a good week. We are very, very sad because Ivar, one of my Canine Companions classmates, died after eating something he shouldn't have.

Ivar was a year-old black Lab-Golden Retriever cross. He was smart, sweet, and happy. His puppy raiser is devastated and inconsolable. The other puppy raisers are mourning his loss as well.

I am loathe to admit it, but dogs, and perhaps Labradors in particular, think anything and everything is edible. We sneak things off counters and tables and other places, knowing we're not supposed to, but oh-so-tempted by something that might be tasty. For example, Hudson once ate a bar of Irish Spring soap from the tray in the bathtub. The good news is that it wasn't fatal or even serious. Marianne called the vet immediately, and Dr. Vicksman told her to watch him closely and bring him in right away if he exhibited certain symptoms (which I won't go into, in case you have a sensitive stomach). Fortunately, Hudson only suffered some ... uh ... minor dietary distress. I'm sure the advertisers of Irish Spring didn't have dog bellies in mind when they coined the phrase "Fresh and clean as a whistle."

But back to more serious things.

Marianne is always on the alert for things that I might try to eat. She is constantly telling me not to eat things off the ground, making me spit things out that I've picked up, and even reaching in and fishing something out of my mouth when I've decided I don't want to spit it out, which annoys me. *Drop* is the command I seem to hear most often.

But now I understand why she does that. Now it makes sense: some things really and truly are deadly. And many things that are fine for humans are lethal to dogs. My friend Ivar snagged a bottle off the counter and ate some vitamin supplements that proved to be toxic to dogs. Sadly, the vet wasn't able to save him.

Marianne keeps hugging me with big tears in her eyes, saying "Ross, PLEASE promise me you won't eat anything unless it's in your dish or an approved training treat." She's warned Meryl and Mina, too. Meryl has an affinity for shoes, and Mina likes things out of the trash. Marianne is making extra sure that anything and everything we might taste, chew, or gulp down is out of reach, out of sight, or both.

We get it, we really do.

Give your pups a hug today and tell them not to eat stuff that's not approved for doggies. And please take the time to look around your house and make sure it is one hundred percent dog-proof. Do it in memory of my friend Ivar.

Chow for now!
Ross

LOST, STOLEN, OR STRAYED

The bad week we are having just got worse.

Our dear Dash Kitty has gone missing. He has the nickname of "Poof!" because he often apparates (I told you we are Harry Potter fans) to another room of the house, but he always APPEARS some place after he turns on the spot and disappears. This time, he's vanished.

We're beside ourselves with worry, and Dewey is especially lonesome. He and Dash are best pals.

Mina, Meryl, and I have helped Marianne and John search inside the house, looking in every cupboard, closet and cranny. Marianne and John have searched outside, around and around the house and the surrounding countryside, in ever-widening circles. They've searched all around the empty house next door in case Dash found a way in but not out. No luck. It breaks my heart to hear them calling, "DASH! DASH KITTY!" and hear no answering meow.

Mina went along on one outdoor excursion, and I went on another. "Find the kitty!" Marianne implored. "Use your super-powerful noses and FIND HIM!" We found all kinds of interesting scents, a couple of bunnies, and lots of birds, but no Dash. Meryl has particularly fine eyesight, so Marianne asked her to keep watch from all available windows. She's seen deer, bunnies, birds and people, but no Dash. All three of us feel terrible that our superpowers have failed to find Dash. He's not an outdoor kitty, so we're worried that he's in danger.

Between looking outside and in, Marianne has filed missing pet reports with several places online. She went to local shelters to look at the cats in their lost and found kennels (no sign of Dash), and she filed Missing Pet Reports at all of them. Marianne has commented more than once that she's glad Dash is microchipped; if he turns up at a shelter they'll know who to call. She and John take turns looking online at all the metro area shelters for buff-colored cats with light green eyes. And then they go outside and call for Dash again.

Marianne and John distributed fliers with Dash's photo to nearby houses last night. The neighbors all said they were sorry and that they'd keep an eye out for Dash. A nice lady at one shelter suggested putting a worn item of clothing outside the door, because sometimes the scent helps a lost animal find its way home. Marianne promptly put t-shirts outside both doors. She also put a crate outside with the door open and fresh water and food, in case he comes home when we're at work and needs a place to hide or rest.

We're all very mindful of the fact that we have many coyotes and foxes in the neighborhood who think house pets are extra-tasty entrees.

"THIS is why you don't go outside!" Marianne snapped at Dewey.

He blinked at her in surprise. "Hey, I'm right here, INSIDE where I belong!"

"You're right. I'm so worried I can't even think straight. I'm sorry." Marianne reached out to rub his chin.

Dewey crawled into her lap. "I know, I'm worried too," he said. "What was he thinking, apparating like that?!"

"Perhaps Dash will be back in time for dinner," I said hopefully.

"Maybe," said Marianne, curling up with Dewey in the window seat overlooking the front yard.

We're waiting for Dash to appear any minute now.

Any.

Minute.

Now.

[sound of clock ticking]

Chow for now!
Ross

FRIDAY FOLLIES

An evening in downtown Denver is always interesting, but last night was especially so. We went with Vanessa and Kevin and their Canine Companions puppy Dennie, first to dinner and then a musical. We parked near the theater and then walked to the restaurant.

On the way we ran into a huge group of men wearing tuxedos and sneakers in front of the Ellie Caulkins Opera House. They were part of a wedding party. "Where are the bride and groom?" wondered Vanessa. One of the fellows gestured toward the street.

We walked a little further and found them on the corner, having their photos taken. We stopped to watch, fascinated by the adorable couple who were leaping into the air off a bench, giggling and making faces for the photographer.

"Gee, I wish we'd had that much fun having our wedding photos taken," said Marianne.

Vanessa boldly asked if they'd mind posing with Dennie and me. They readily agreed and told us we were quite handsome as Vanessa snapped our picture with her cell phone. The professional photographers took a couple pictures too, so we might end up in their wedding album. Wouldn't that be funny? Off we went to dinner, where Dennie and I napped under the table. I have no idea why we couldn't have had chiles rellenos too, but Marianne told me quite firmly, "NO." Huh.

As we were walking to the theater after dinner we ran into a large group of oddly-dressed and very enthusiastic people. Turns out they were dressed as gladiators, doing a charity pub crawl for another service dog organization! Small world, no? They were delighted to pose with us for a photo, too.

Dennie and I settled in for a nice nap once the play started, enjoying the music and ignoring the rest of it. The first act was pretty long though, and I got really hot so I stood up to see what was happening on stage. I was so happy I started wagging my tail, accidentally whacking the two nice ladies in the seats in front of John. (Those seats in the theater are kind of close together! The designer didn't think about service dogs.) The ladies were very nice about it and just laughed at me. I climbed into Marianne's lap and panted loudly to make sure she knew I was hot. The lady in front of Marianne turned around with a startled look on her face—I guess she thought it was Marianne making the loud panting noise. She smiled when she realized it was me. Marianne, however, was not amused.

"Ross, hush!" she hissed. "I know you're warm but you'll just have to wait until intermission for a drink of water." I tried to pant more quietly as I watched the action on stage for the remainder of the first act.

At intermission we went outside for some fresh air, a *hurry* break and a drink of water. What a relief! The second act was shorter, and Dennie and I snoozed through it. In fact, Marianne had to jostle me awake. I was so relaxed that I slept through thunderous applause and two curtain calls!

Just an average evening in the life of a puppy in training.

Chow for now!
Ross

STILL MISSING

Our kitty Dash is still missing and my family is very sad. We've spent a lot of time walking around the property and the surrounding neighborhoods, going to shelters in person and looking at shelters online for Dash, but so far no luck.

It about kills Marianne to go to the shelters in person because she wants to bring all the kitties home with us. "Well, why not?" I asked. "Why not adopt another kitty? I'll help you pick one out!"

"We will adopt another cat, especially since Dewey is so lonesome for Dash," Marianne assured me, "but I'm not quite ready yet. I'm still hoping that Dash will come home."

"So, we'll have THREE kitties if Dash comes home. Won't that be great?" I wagged my tail hopefully.

"HA," Marianne snorted. "Talk to John. He says that two cats and two keeper dogs plus one Canine Companions puppy in training is plenty for our family, and he's probably right. Besides, what would Dash think if he came home and there was a new kitty here?"

Oh, I hadn't thought of that. I bet his feelings would be hurt. Oh, Dash – COME HOME!

Chow for now!
Ross

JOYFUL DOG TRIXIE

Today's the day! Bestselling author Dean Koontz has published his first non-fiction book, and it's about his beloved Trixie. *A Big Little Life: Memoir of a Joyful Dog* hits the bookstores today. I can't wait to read it. Trixie was a Canine Companions service dog who retired early for medical reasons. She adopted Dean and Gerda Koontz, and their lives were never the same.

Now, you may be thinking that I wrote that sentence backwards, that I really meant to say that Dean and Gerda adopted Trixie, but of course it was the other way around. She had big plans, Trixie did. She changed Dean and Gerda's perceptions of animals and the animal-human bond. She made sure that Canine Companions became an important part of their lives, to the extent that they have donated millions of dollars to the organization; the Southwest Regional Center is now called the Dean, Gerda and Trixie Koontz Campus.

Living with a prolific writer influenced Trixie, too. She wrote three books of her own: *Life is Good: Lessons in Joyful Living, Christmas is Good,* and *Bliss to You.* I highly recommend all of them. Trixie had a wicked sense of humor, which is sometimes necessary when dealing with humans. She was also wise and insightful. All proceeds from Trixie's books and *A Big Little Life* are donated to Canine Companions for Independence. How wonderful is that?

Sadly, Trixie passed away in the summer of 2007, but her joyful spirit lives on. Hmmm, maybe if I get released from the program I could go live with Dean and Gerda?

Chow for now!
Ross

DOZER

Marianne and I were driving home from running some errands Wednesday morning and I said, "Let's stop by the Dumb Friends League and look at cats!"

Marianne caught my eye in the rear view mirror. "We are thinking about another kitty, but I hadn't planned on doing anything this week."

"I know," I said. "But I just have a feeling. Let's go look today."

She shrugged and said, "OK, we're not far from the League and we have time. Why not?"

A few minutes later we pulled into the parking lot. Marianne snapped on my leash, and we walked in the front door. "Look, kittens! They're so cute!" I exclaimed, pulling Marianne over to a glass display.

Marianne pulled me gently back. "No Ross, kittens are not for us. Let's look at the older cats."

"Look at that little gray one! And the orange one! They are so playful! I want one!"

Marianne pulled me to the side. "Ross, *sit*. There are several reasons why a kitten isn't what we are looking for. First of all, we have a very large dog who doesn't know how big she is. Meryl would not intentionally hurt a kitten but she might accidentally step on it or play too roughly with it."

This is true: Meryl has accidentally stepped on my paws and galloped over me in the yard and she is always surprised when I yelp.

"Second," Marianne continued, "kittens always get adopted. For some reason, people don't want to adopt the older cats, which is silly. Even if a cat is seven or eight years old, it still has many years to be a wonderful companion."

I looked longingly at the kittens and sighed. "All right, I see your point. Let's look at the older kitties."

We stopped at a kiosk, and Marianne started typing on a keyboard. I nudged her arm. "Why are you doing that?"

"This is the way the League collects information on our family and what kind of pet we're interested in adopting. We are looking for an older male cat who gets along with other cats and dogs. There, that's done. Now we can go look."

We walked up to the desk, and three nice employees all said hello and made a fuss over me. Marianne explained that she wanted to look at the cats.

"Sure, go right through those doors," said one lady. "But Ross can't go in with you. Can he stay out here with us?"

Marianne looked relieved. "That would be great, thank you!"

"Let me know who you pick!" I barked as she walked away.

The League ladies petted me and made me demonstrate my commands. They gave me a few treats for being a good boy and rubbed my tummy. Someone walked up, pulling a cart with several carriers on it.

"Oooh, Ziggy's back from foster care!" exclaimed one of the ladies. "Say, he'd be a good fit for your family, Ross. He was fostered in a home with dogs and cats, so we know he gets along with everyone." She pulled the largest carrier off the cart and her knees buckled slightly. I looked in but all I saw was a huge mound of fur. She half carried, half dragged the carrier to a nearby room and shut the door while one of the other employees went to find Marianne.

"Can I meet Ziggy?" I asked the remaining employee.

She shook her head. "Let's see what Marianne thinks of him first."

Just then I saw Marianne and the other employee go into the room where Ziggy was and shut the door. I heard laughter. Lots of laughter. After a bit Marianne came out.

"Well?" I demanded. "What's he like? Is he our kitty?"

She smiled. "Yes, I think so. I am going to talk to John this evening, and if he agrees I'll come back to adopt Ziggy tomorrow."

I told the ladies goodbye and we left. Marianne refused to tell me anything more about Ziggy, only that he was very friendly and would be a good match for our family. Huh.

The next day I went to work with John. When we got home Marianne wasn't there. Soon I heard the car pull up, and she came in the house.

John met her at the door. "Did you get the cat?"

"Yes, he's in the car. Can you bring him in?" Marianne shooed Meryl and Mina into the master bedroom and shut the door. "You can see him in a few minutes," she told them.

John walked in lugging a medium-size dog crate, which he took into the guest room, shutting the door in my face.

"HEY!" I protested.

"Ross, back off," Marianne said. "Let them get acquainted first. Remember how we did this when we adoted Dewey."

Dewey joined me at the door and meowed loudly. "Yeah, I know what you mean," I grumbled. Marianne opened the bedroom door and Meryl and Mina skidded to a stop in front of the guest room. I filled them in on the situation as we sat in front of the door, hoping for a glimpse of Ziggy. Marianne took in some food and a litter box.

After a while John came out. "Good choice," he told us.

Marianne came out and put a baby gate in front of the door. "You can look at each other for now," she said. "We'll work up to face-to-face introductions gradually." We peered into the room, looking for a cat.

"Where's Ziggy?" I asked. "All I see is a fur blanket on the bed."

"That *is* Ziggy," Marianne laughed.

I blinked. "No way, that's not a cat. He's HUGE. He's bigger than Mina." Mina whimpered and took a step back. Meryl cocked her head and wagged her tail happily. Finally, a cat big enough for her to play with.

"Yeah, that's why he was in foster care," Marianne said. "He was thirty-two pounds when he arrived at the League in July but he's lost eight pounds. We'll help him lose a few more."

Ziggy lashed his tail and growled at Meryl, who was moaning at him. "Meryl, I keep telling you, cats don't think that's funny," Marianne scolded her. Meryl grinned and moaned louder. Dewey glared at her and jumped over the gate. He cautiously approached Ziggy. They stared at each other for a minute, then Dewey jumped on the bed and curled up near Ziggy. Both cats purred loudly.

"Are you going to call him Ziggy?" I asked. "What about a name beginning with D?"

"Your Auntie Diane suggested Dozer, short for bulldozer. John says that Ziggy Marley's real name was David. I think we're going to call him Dozer Dave. He's such a big kitty, he needs two names." She moved the baby gate and shut the door. "Let's let him relax for a bit, OK?"

"OK," I said. "But I still don't believe anything that big is a house cat. Mountain lion, maybe."

Chow for now!
Ross

TREVIN

I have some very sad news to tell you this week. Marianne's first Canine Companions puppy, my Great Uncle Trevin, has gone to the Rainbow Bridge, as the puppy raisers say. He was eight years old. He died from complications of cancer.

I never met Trevin, but this is what I know from the many conversations I've overheard:

Trevin came to Denver as an eight-week-old puppy and walked right into Marianne and John's hearts. He immediately made friends with the pets in the house, including the cats, and settled into the family routine as though he'd never lived anywhere else. He learned his commands quickly and easily, didn't eat anything he wasn't supposed to, behaved perfectly in public, and charmed everyone he knew.

After Trevin went to professional training in Oceanside, and Marianne and John were raising their second puppy—nicknamed "Stryker No, Stryker Don't,"—Marianne was heard to remark, "Oh, I get it now. Canine Companions sends you the perfect puppy the first time and suckers you into the program, and then they send you the challenging puppy!"

Trevin had charisma. Even people who weren't fond of dogs would melt at his soulful gaze and reach down to pet him. Invariably someone would say, "He looks so sad!" Marianne would laugh and reply, "Yes, he practices that look in the mirror so you'll come over and pet him. It worked, didn't it?"

In fact, Trevin was a very happy dog who loved to play, but he took his work very seriously. When his cape was on, he was a Working Dog. He loved to be petted, but he always obeyed the rules and sat calmly, with one notable exception. Any time Trevin saw Dave Green, 7News Director, he would break his *sit-stay* and gallop over to Dave, jump up, and cover his face with kisses. Marianne was horrified every time this happened, but Trevin persisted despite sharp corrections. Fortunately, Dave was a Dog Person and loved Trevin in equal measure. Dave passed away in September of 2006, and Marianne is certain that Dave is the first person Trevin looked for in heaven.

Trevin did very well in professional training, but as the training intensified he became anxious and began to exhibit signs of stress, such as barking in public. Canine Companions has very high standards, and the first priority is always the safety of the human and canine team. An anxious, stressed dog is not a solid working dog. Trevin's trainer worked with him to overcome his fears, but in the end they made the difficult decision to release him from the program the day before Team Training began.

Because Marianne and John already had two pet dogs, and because they felt Trevin wanted to be more than a house pet, they asked Canine Companions to place Trevin with their friend Carol, who was interested in adopting a released dog to participate in pet therapy programs. This seemed like a perfect match for Trevin, who loved to work, just not full time. Carol and Trevin became a certified therapy team.Trevin was a tolerant fellow, submitting to ridiculous costumes, for example—he understood that therapy takes many forms, including making people smile.

Trevin wasn't all work, however. He enjoyed traveling, attending baseball games, and playing with his favorite toy, Ducky. He never tried to field dress or otherwise play too roughly with Ducky. Marianne and John passed it along to Carol, and despite receiving a grand assortment of toys, including stuffed ducks, over the years, Ducky remained Trevin's favorite. When small holes appeared in Ducky from time to time, Trevin watched anxiously as Carol made the necessary repairs. He often used it as a pillow during his morning sunbath and nap in Carol's backyard.

When Trevin was diagnosed with cancer, everyone hoped for a positive outcome, but it wasn't to be. Trevin was buried with Ducky.

I'm sorry I never got to meet Trevin, but I am glad I have his legacy to follow.

Chow for now.
Ross

MARS

MARS IS COMING TO DENVER ON NOVEMBER 18.

That got your attention, didn't it? But which Mars?

Mars the planet? Mars the candy company? Mars the Roman god of war? Mars the melodic death metal rock band?

Nope. Give up? The answer is: Mars the puppy!

Mars will be puppy #7 for John and Marianne (and 7News, of course). He's a black Labrador and Golden Retriever cross. His father, Blaze, is a Golden Retriever, and his mother, Nyrobi, is three-quarters Lab, one-quarter Golden, which makes Mars ... um ... [sounds of calculator keys] carry the 2 add 6 times 45 divided by 8 plus pi ... um ... five-eighths Golden and three-eighths Lab.

I think.

Anyhow, Mars is the "red" puppy, which means he was born first. He's also big, fluffy (!), and very cuddly, according to Marti, Nyrobi's Canine Companions breeder caretaker. Marti said, "Nyrobi is very sweet and loves to play. She was an attentive mother for the first few weeks but was very happy to turn the feeding over to us (humans) this past Tuesday. The pups took to the weaning food immediately; they are good eaters."

I think that's the Lab part, myself. You'll never meet a Lab who doesn't love to eat.

Marti also said of the pups, "They all seem to be quick learners and they are a very affectionate group. Mars is particularly interested in a rubber dumbbell that is in the playpen. He likes to put his front paw on it and roll it back and forth. He is a cutie!"

Marianne is already besotted with him and he's not even here yet. Yeesh.

I'll be at professional training when Mars arrives, so I won't get to meet him, but I'm OK with that. I won't have to listen to everyone at 7News make a big fuss over how cute he is. I won't have to wait my turn to be noticed, let alone petted. I also won't have to babysit or share my favorite toy or teach him the house rules. HA! The cats and keeper dogs can do those things.

Stay tuned for more details.

Chow for now!
Ross

BONNY PRINCE ROSS

We have a blanket at my house that has a name. It's called The MacDuff. Marianne pulled it out of the closet last night because she was cold and wanted something to snuggle into while watching the news. I jumped on the sofa and offered to sit in her lap but she snapped, "Ross, off!" Jeez. I was just trying to help keep her warm.

Anyhow, Meryl curled up on the sofa next to Marianne (keeper dogs, different rules, bah humbug) and asked why the blanket had a name. "Is it because it's this pretty plaid?" she wondered. "All your other blankets are plain colors."

"Well yes," Marianne said. "This is called a tartan, and in Scotland tartans are associated with specific family names, like MacDuff."

"Or RRRoss," I added, rolling the 'r' to give it the proper Scottish lilt.

Marianne looked at me in surprise. "Now how did you know that?"

"Jennie RRRoss tauld me all aboot it, ye ken," I said smugly.

"Who is Jennie Ross?" interrupted Meryl.

"She's a photo journalist at 7News," Marianne explained. She turned back to me. "And why are you talking like that? Do you have something caught in your throat?"

"Dinnae fash yersel," I said airly. "I bin studyin' a wee bit."

Marianne looked at me warily. "Studying what, exactly?"

"Th' clan, o'coorse. Crivens, woman! Ah'm a RRRoss!" I barked.

"I see," said Marianne. "I'm just guessing, but have you been using the Nac Mac Feegles from Terry Pratchett's Discworld books as your language tutors?"

"Och aye, they ur guid teachers ," I said. "Ah am prood tae wear th' RRRoss tartan, ye ken."

"And do you even 'ken' what the Ross tartan looks like?" Marianne inquired, rather too politely.

I trotted over to my cape and pulled out two scarves from the pocket. "Aye, Jennie RRRoss lent me these. Th' green is th' huntin' tartan."

Marianne laughed and draped the scarves around my neck. "Awe rite, ye win," she said, reaching for the camera. "Bonny Prince Ross," she declared, snapping my picture.

Haste ye back (and Chow for now!)
Ross

A MATTER OF TRUST

Tuesday was my last day at 7News. On Thursday I am flying to Oceanside with Marianne and John for professional training, or "turn-in," as they call it, on Saturday. Billy Joel was warbling away on the car radio as we drove home Tuesday night. "It's always been a matter of trust," he sang. Marianne parked the car in the driveway and sat for a minute looking thoughtful.

"What?" I asked. "Don't you like that song?"

"I do," she replied, "But I've been thinking about turn-in, and that song made me think about the concept of trust. A lot of what happens at Canine Companions is about trust, when you think about it."

We got out of the car and headed into the house, where we were mobbed by Meryl and Mina and the cats in the usual greeting frenzy. Later, after dinner and play time, I followed Marianne into the bedroom.

"What did you mean when you said Canine Companions was about trust?" I asked.

She sat down in the rocking chair and pulled me into her lap for some cradling time. "Well, every part of Canine Companions relates to and depends on every other part, and all of it requires a certain amount of trust."

I squirmed into a more comfortable position. "Explain, please."

Marianne rubbed my ears. "Well, for example, people who donate money trust that Canine Companions will be good stewards of their donations and use the money to further the goals of the program." She began massaging my front paws. "Another example is the volunteer breeder caretakers. Canine Companions requires them to live near the NW campus in Santa Rosa and to care for the breeder dogs. That means keeping the males in excellent physical health and being available to take them to campus on short notice for `dates'. It means keeping the females in excellent physical health, caring for them during their pregnancies, and then caring for the puppies until they are eight weeks old, which involves a lot of cleaning, record keeping, and other tasks to begin socializing the puppies."

I thought about it. "And then the puppies go to their volunteer puppy raisers, right?"

Marianne nodded. "Yup, and Canine Companions trusts us to keep you safe, in good health, teach you about thirty basic commands and love the stuffing out of you. But more than that, they trust us to remember that you're not pets, and to follow their rules. Plus, we're entrusted with taking puppies out appropriately in public and being good ambassadors for Canine Companions wherever we go."

"And when we hand the pups back at turn-in, we're trusting that the trainers and staff will love you as much as we do. When we handed over Trevin, I was sure that no one could love him as much as I did, but when I saw him six months later with his trainer, Simi, I knew I was wrong. Boy, was I wrong," she laughed. "It was very clear when I saw them together that he adored her and she loved him like crazy."

I stretched. "Were you a little sad or jealous?"

"No, I was delighted, and that's part of the Canine Companions magic. We learn to open our hearts in so many ways," Marianne said, rubbing my tummy. I groaned happily.

"What else?" I asked.

"The people who have applied for dogs trust that the trainers will match them with a canine partner who will become their key to greater independence. That's a huge leap of faith, especially for someone who has never had a pet dog before, much less an assistance dog, and isn't really sure how the dog will help or how things will work out."

"It's kind of like an arranged marriage, huh? You hope you fall in love, but what if it's awful?" I mused.

Marianne stopped rubbing my tummy. "Have you been reading romance novels again?" she asked.

I blushed. "Maybe one or two. But how do the trainers know the match will work out?"

"Part of it is their experience with the dogs; after six or nine months of training they know the particular skills of each dog really well. And the staff who interview the applicants work closely with the trainers so they know what kind of assistance each person will need from a Canine Companions dog." She gently pushed me off her lap and stood up.

I wagged my tail. "And the trainers and staff trust that the graduates will love the dogs and treat them well and call Canine Companions if they need anything, right?"

"Right," Marianne agreed. "It's a circle."

I pondered for a moment. "So the circle starts all over again when I go to turn-in on Saturday and you get Mars next week, doesn't it?"

Marianne hugged me and her voice sounded a little shaky. "Yes, it does. It's one of the things that makes this such a bittersweet experience." She wiped her eyes. "Now, let's go get your bedtime cookie. We have a very early flight tomorrow."

Wish me luck on the next phase of my training!

Chow for now and love,
Ross

MARS

THE NEW
BREED

Mars arrived in Denver via Alaska Airlines on November 18, 2009. Jeannie (Parker's human) and I picked him up late in the afternoon. He was, shall we say, *very* aromatic. Thank goodness for the puppy room in the cargo terminal! Jeannie bathed Mars while I swabbed out the crate. We gave him a quick snack and a drink before heading home. As is our custom, the Denver Village showed up to welcome the newest arrival with presents for the new puppy and pizza for the humans.

Mars was what Canine Companions people call a "rare black fluffy." He looked like a black Golden Retriever. Everyone asked: "What kind of dog is that?" He had long, black wavy fur, soulful eyes, and curly spaniel ears. He had golden fur showing through on his legs and feet; we called it his gold dust. Mars was a three-hour grocery store dog, meaning we didn't take him if we wanted to get through a shopping trip in under three hours, because everyone would want to stop to chat about him.

Mars was the most sociable of the pups we've raised, by far. He was a total love sponge, climbing into our laps for a hug, often while wubbing on his favorite stuffed teddy bear. Mars preferred to hang out with humans all the time; at nine weeks he could scale the four-foot sides of the wire x-pen like a monkey in order to join us wherever we were in the house. When crated he complained loudly at being separated from his human pack. His favorite place to hang out was *under* the bed, even when he had to smash himself flat to crawl under it.

Mars was rock solid in public, though, never startled or freaked out by anything. He was happy to go anywhere and do anything, from an exercise class to a movie to grocery shopping to an airplane trip.

After his teddy bear, Mars' favorite toy was a tennis ball. Mars would stalk tennis players at the gym because he knew they would have tennis balls in their gym bags; it was rather embarrassing. He could hardly bear to walk down the hall by the tennis courts because we would make him leave the stray balls. If I whispered "Mars, tennis ball," he would come at a gallop. The only place we found we could successfully hide tennis balls from him was the refrigerator.

Mars was such a different puppy from our previous six, partly because of his unusual appearance, partly due to his extremely social nature, and partly because of his precocious retrieving skills. At nine weeks he stunned us by picking up a dropped envelope on his own and carrying it a half-block back to the house, never dropping it, chewing it or even slobbering on it. He absolutely loved to carry things: shoes, keys, lunch bag, mail, water bottle ... anything. Every morning he pranced into the lobby at work with something in his mouth and paraded around the room so everyone could ooh and aah at his cleverness.

The new pup wasn't the only one who was different; I'm afraid I was also a very different puppy raiser. Mars arrived while we were in the midst of caring for my mother as she succumbed to cancer, and much of the first two months that he was with us is lost to me, either because of obvious distractions, or because he was being cared for by the Denver Village as we drove or flew back and forth to Albuquerque. We took Mars with us at Thanksgiving, and I will remember with great fondness my mom's happiness as she petted him. "He's so soft!" she kept saying. He was a welcome addition to our family, providing smiles and silliness when we most needed it, keeping us firmly grounded in the present.

MARS' DOGBLOG

HERE WE GO AGAIN: GUEST BLOGGER MERYL FILLS IN WHILE MARS GETS SETTLED

Pssst, Meryl here. I'm writing to let you know that Mars (or as I call him: "He Who Makes Weird Noises and Gets All the Attention") arrived safe and sound on Wednesday. He flew to Denver from San Francisco, wherever that is.

This is my first time through the cycle of turning in one puppy and getting the next one. Marianne explained that Ross was going to professional training and that another Canine Companions puppy named Mars would be coming to live with us. What she neglected to mention is that Mars is only eight weeks old. I was expecting a puppy the size of Ross that I could play with, but NOOOOO. Marianne brought home a little yodeling ball of black fluff, not a puppy. I know Canine Companions puppies. This is not a puppy.

I don't know what I'm supposed to do with this little monster. He's underfoot, and Marianne keeps warning me not to step on him. He chews on my ears and my toes with razor-sharp teeth. He bounces at the cats and gets hissed at a lot. And then there's the Puppy Opera: he howls and yodels and warbles and yips and yaps and shrieks when he's put in his crate for a nap or bedtime. He's so loud that I have to put my paws over my ears! How something that small can make that much noise is deeply puzzling.

He's not even housebroken! He has to go outside constantly. If I ask to go outside that often Marianne tells me to forget it and to go lie down. But the monster only needs to look at the back door or walk around in circles and he's outside. Marianne doesn't even make him walk to the door; she scoops him up and carries him! She explained that small puppies have small bladders, and even smaller attention spans, so the only way to get him outside before he *hurries* is to carry him. I think he's scamming her.

Marianne says he's just a baby and has been through a pretty tough week and that he will settle down. She said that soon enough he'll settle in his crate without the Puppy Opera and that he'll sleep through the night. Yeah? So when am I supposed to get my beauty sleep until then? I notice that Marianne is looking pretty tired herself, so Fuzzbuns better settle down quick. Marianne gets cranky when she doesn't get enough sleep.

yawn Speaking of sleep, I think I'll go take a nap.

Your sleep-deprived correspondent,
Meryl (for Mars)

O BROTHER, WHERE ART THOU?

I keep hearing how amazing it is that I can step right in where Ross left off on the DogBlog. People think I'm too young or something. Well, let me remind everyone that I'm from the new generation of Canine Companions puppies. We're savvy, we're hip, we're techno geeks, we're CC iPups! So there. I am Puppy, watch me Tweet. Hahahahahaha.

Anyhow, I was happy to get a text from my brother Madden this week. We're both big fluffy black puppies with gold splotches on our paws, but Madden has lots more gold mixed in with his fluffy black fur, and golden brown eyebrows. When people ask what I am, Marianne says that I am a "Black and Tan Teddy Bear Retriever," which fits Madden perfectly too.

Madden and I had a good old-fashioned Skype session to fill each other in on our puppy raisers (we call them "PRs"), new homes, family members, and such. It was great to see his furry face!

Turns out, we're leading parallel lives. So many similarities! He lives in the mountains of New Jersey; I live near the Rockies in Colorado. Neither of us gets access to many rooms in our houses, and we each have a long hallway that we enjoy galloping down to get to our crates. (We did find one major difference: while my motto is "H8 the cr8!" Madden says he doesn't mind his crate at all. Huh.)

We agreed that snow was quite a surprise and so fun to play in. Both of us are the first "black fluffy" pups for our PRs. We both like snuggling with our PRs, and we like being told we're the Cutest Puppies EVER by everyone we meet.

You'd think we were littermates or something! Oh, wait—we are!

Chow for now!
Mars

P.S. Cool coincidence: Madden's PRs, Regina and Dave, also raised Parker's sister, Patrina!

TWELVE DOGS OF CHRISTMAS

I've been listening to a lot of Christmas carols lately and I have to say I am surprised at how few mention dogs. Why is that, I wonder? I know most people would rather sing about dogs than snowmen or reindeer or chestnuts or holly or jingle bells. Jeez.

Anyhow, I thought I'd try updating a song for you so you can sing about dogs this Christmas. Consider it my gift to you!

The Twelve Dogs of Christmas
By Mars

The first dog of Christmas, the shelter sent to me?
An Airedale with a bad knee.

The second dog of Christmas, the shelter sent to
     me?
Two bashful Borzois,
And an Airedale with a bad knee.

The third dog of Christmas, the shelter sent to me?
Three chubby Chows,
Two bashful Borzois,
And an Airedale with a bad knee.

The fourth dog of Christmas, the shelter sent to me?
Four daffy Danes,
Three chubby Chows,
Two bashful Borzois,
And an Airedale with a bad knee.

The fifth dog of Christmas, the shelter sent to me?
Five Gold-a-doodles!
Four daffy Danes,
Three chubby Chows,
Two bashful Borzois,
And an Airedale with a bad knee.

The sixth dog of Christmas, the shelter sent to me?
Six Greyhounds grinning,
Five Gold-a-doodles!
Four daffy Danes,

Three chubby Chows,
Two bashful Borzois,
And an Airedale with a bad knee.

The seventh dog of Christmas, the shelter sent to me?
Seven Spitz a-sneezing,
Six Greyhounds grinning,
Five Gold-a-doodles!
Four daffy Danes,
Three chubby Chows,
Two bashful Borzois,
And an Airedale with a bad knee.

The eighth dog of Christmas, the shelter sent to me?
Eight Pugs a-piddling,
Seven Spitz a-sneezing,
Six Greyhounds grinning,
Five Gold-a-doodles!
Four daffy Danes,
Three chubby Chows,
Two bashful Borzois,
And an Airedale with a bad knee.

The ninth dog of Christmas, the shelter sent to me?
Nine Poodles prancing,
Eight Pugs a-piddling,
Seven Spitz a-sneezing,
Six Greyhounds grinning,
Five Gold-a-doodles!
Four daffy Danes,
Three chubby Chows,
Two bashful Borzois,
And an Airedale with a bad knee.

The tenth dog of Christmas, the shelter sent to me?
Ten Labs a-leaping,
Nine Poodles prancing,
Eight Pugs a-piddling,

Seven Spitz a-sneezing,
Six Greyhounds grinning,
Five Gold-a-doodles!
Four daffy Danes,
Three chubby Chows,
Two bashful Borzois,
And an Airedale with a bad knee.

The eleventh dog of Christmas, the shelter sent to me?
Eleven Schnauzers snoozing,
Ten Labs a-leaping,
Nine Poodles prancing,
Eight Pugs a-piddling,
Seven Spitz a-sneezing,
Six Greyhounds grinning,
Five Gold-a-doodles!
Four daffy Danes,
Three chubby Chows,
Two bashful Borzois,
And an Airedale with a bad knee.

[Deep breath now, big finish!]
The twelfth day of Christmas, the shelter sent to me:
Twelve dozen poop bags,
Eleven Schnauzers snoozing,
Ten Labs a-leaping,
Nine Poodles prancing,
Eight Pugs a-piddling,
Seven Spitz a-sneezing,
Six Greyhounds grinning,
Five Gold-a-doodles!
Four daffy Danes,
Three chubby Chows,
Two bashful Borzois,
And an Airedale with a bad knee!

Happy Christmas to all!
Mars

DEAR OLD DAD

My Dad's name is Blaze. I never met him, but I heard he's a great guy. Still, I wondered what he was like, so Marianne found his email address and I sent him a note yesterday. I asked him where he grew up, where he lives now and what that's like, and how many puppies he has sired. I wondered how he was chosen to be a breeder for Canine Companions. And most of all, I'm curious to know if I am like him at all.

Well, he sent me a reply right away. I was so excited when Marianne told me to come read his note that I almost forgot to finish my lunch.

Almost.

First things first, after all.

Here's his letter. Marianne says she can tell where I get my sense of humor, my need for constant affection, and my precocious ability to carry things like her car keys.

Dear Mars,

> *Thanks for your email of January 12. It is always great to hear from one of my kids; so few of you write. You'd think that with 56, somebody would lift up a paw and send a card.*

> *Since you asked, I wanted to give you some information on myself. You can pass it along if you want or you can write an article about me for the* New Yorker. *Your call, puppy.*

> *I was born on March 27, 2004, in Santa Rosa, California. I was raised in Snohomish, Washington, and repatriated to Canine Companions Headquarters in Santa Rosa when I was about 14 months old, for graduate school. I know it seems a little young for grad school, but I was, as they say, precocious. A couple of months later, I was selected to be a "breeder." (Tell 'em your old man is a professional breeder, Mars, and believe me—you'll get respect.)*

In October, 2005, Canine Companions started to look for a caretaker for me (a home, if you will). It didn't take long. Potential caretakers were lined up for miles. After some tough questioning on my part, I selected Linda and Allen Jackson. They had a big yard, a pond for swimming, and the house had been freshly painted. I like that. Additionally, there was a gorgeous blonde golden retriever already living there; she was just about my age and quite a looker. Her name is Lizzie. I hope you do as well, kid.

Despite my undying love for Lizzie, I have had about 10 dates with other breeder girls at Canine Companions — it's what I do. These dates have led to 56 children, with more on the way. That's a lot of brothers, sisters, half-brothers, and half-sisters for you, sport.

When my friends and relatives are asked "What makes Blaze such a great dog?" they usually mention that I have a great sense of humor, an ability to speak several languages (none of which is intelligible), and an insatiable desire to provide affection, receive affection, carry almost anything, and retrieve the newspaper every morning with great gusto. Reading the paper has been a bit of a challenge for me, but I'm working on it.

I don't know what you want to do with your life, Mars, but I've given you the best genes that I have. The rest is up to you. Be good to those who love you. Don't growl without a real good reason. And, above all, keep in touch.

Always,
Dad

WOW. I mean, how great is he? I hope I grow up to be as charismatic and funny and smart as my dad!

Chow for now!
Mars

BEST OF THE BEST

Yesterday morning I was napping peacefully under Marianne's desk when the phone rang. That happens a lot, and I didn't think anything of it until Marianne began jumping up and down.

"Hey!" I protested, "I get scolded when I jump around like that."

"Oh Mars, I am so happy!" she exclaimed, hanging up the phone. "That was Stu. He was calling to let us know that Ross has been chosen for the breeding program!"

I jumped up and down a couple of times myself. "Wow, that is great news, just like my Dad, Blaze!" I sat down and scratched my ear. " Um, how does that work, exactly?"

Marianne collapsed into her chair and opened up the Canine Companions web site on her computer. "OK, you know that Canine Companions has its own breeding program. They breed Labradors, Golden Retrievers, and crosses of the two (like you). In order to explain just how big a deal it is to be chosen, I'm going to quote Canine Companions." She peered at the computer screen and read: "'Our breeding program staff checks each dog's temperament, trainability, health, physical attributes, littermate trends, and the production history of the dam and sire. Only then are the best of the best chosen as Canine Companions breeder dogs.'" She sighed happily.

"Mercy, that is impressive," I agreed. "Good old Ross, The Best of the Best. What happens next?"

"Just like your dad, Ross will live with a breeder caretaker near Santa Rosa and enjoy a very nice life in between dates with Canine Companions girl dogs at the Northwest campus. It's even possible that we might be able to meet his breeder caretaker and visit Ross some day."

"Will you be able to raise a Ross puppy?" I asked.

"Possibly," Marianne said. "We will request one and then we'll just have to wait and see." She pulled me into her lap for a hug. "But that won't happen for a long time because we have you to love until May of 2011!"

Chow for now!
Mars

BOBBY THE GREAT

Speaking of the best of the best, the greatest of the greats, we received news that Bobby, a renowned Canine Companions breeder, passed away last weekend. He was a once-in-a-lifetime dog and will be missed by the entire Canine Companions family, especially his breeder caretakers, M-L* and Bill.

Bobby was raised in the Northeast Region and was selected for the Canine Companions breeder program in 1997. He sired over 750 puppies during his career; 40 became breeder dogs, and 230 graduated as expertly trained assistance dogs for adults and children with disabilities.

Over 3,300 Canine Companions dogs are related in some way to Bobby, including ME! He was my great-grandfather on my mother's side. In fact, every one of Marianne's Canine Companions pups is related to Bobby. Trevin was his son; Stryker, Hudson, and Ross are grandsons; Rolly was a great grandson, and Parker is a great nephew.

Marianne says that when she and John attended their very first puppy class with Trevin, one of the other puppy raisers asked who Trevin's parents were. Marianne said, "I can't remember his mom's name, but I think his father is called Bobby." She said there was a collective intake of breath and then a chorus of "Oooh, a BOBBY puppy!" She and John had an inkling that Trevin might be a very special puppy indeed.

As my Auntie Elizabeth said "It's the end of an era, but not the end of a dynasty."

Rest in peace, Bobby. You will be sorely missed.

Chow for now.
Mars

My imagination always runs away with me when I hear the famous M-L's name. What could it be? "Mighty Lovely"? Text me if you know.

TUTORED!

Marianne was on the phone with another puppy raiser. I was mostly asleep until I heard my name. Marianne said "Yes, Mars is going to see Dr. Vicksman this week to get tutored."

When she hung up I crawled out from under the desk and stretched, then put my head in her lap for a pat. "Why am I going to see Dr. Vicksman?" I yawned. "You said he was going to tutor me, but Amy is our puppy class teacher. Is Dr. V. teaching Canine Companions classes now?"

Marianne gently rubbed my ears. "Um, no, Dr. Vicksman is not actually going to tutor you." She reached over and pulled a cartoon off the bulletin board. "I was repeating the punch line in this cartoon."

In the Far Side cartoon, one dog is wagging his tail as he leans out a car window. He's talking to another dog who is sitting on the lawn. The caption reads, "Ha ha ha, Biff. Guess what? After we go to the drug store and the post office, I'm going to the vet's to get tutored!"

I shook my head. "I don't get it," I said.

"It's a play on words," Marianne explained. "The dog misunderstood his human, who actually said the dog was going to the vet to get neutered, not tutored."

I re-read the caption. "Oh, now I get it," I snickered. "Yeah, OK, I see why that's funny." I started to crawl under the desk to go back to my nap when it hit me.

"Hold it! Wait just a kibble-crunching minute!" I exclaimed. "You said I was going to the vet to get tutored but you meant NEUTERED, didn't you?" I stared at Marianne in horror. "I don't feel well," I moaned, putting my head between my paws.

"Oh, Mars, we talked about this before. Don't panic." Marianne scooped me into her lap. "Oof. Jeez, you're huge! How much do you weigh now?"

"Around sixty pounds, and don't try to change the subject," I snapped. "You could give a puppy a little notice about things like this."

Marianne rubbed my tummy. "Oh, stop being so dramatic. The surgery is very quick, and by the next day you'll feel just fine."

I twisted my head around to stare at her. "The NEXT day? What about Wednesday? How am I going to feel on Wednesday?" I had a feeling I wasn't going to like the answer.

Marianne kissed my nose and said, "You won't feel anything during the surgery, but you'll probably be a little woozy afterwards from the anesthetic. Your incision may be a little painful. Dr. Vicksman will give you some medication that will help."

"My INCISION?" I wailed. "This is worse than I thought!"

"Now you're just being silly." Marianne abruptly set me back down on the floor. "Look, your friend Calhoun had the surgery last month and he was fine, wasn't he?"

"Yeah, I guess so," I said slowly. "I don't think he mentioned it, actually."

Marianne briskly patted my head. "There you go. He was back in class and playing with you and the other pups, and you didn't even know he'd had the surgery. You'll be just fine."

She hesitated. "Oh, there is one other thing I should tell you. You won't get breakfast on Wednesday morning."

I gasped. "But WHY? I'll be hungry, I'm always starving when we get up in the morning! You know that! No food AND surgery?" I whimpered softly.

Marianne rolled her eyes. "Look, it's not safe for you to have food before surgery. It's the same for humans. I promise you'll have dinner on Wednesday."

"Can I have something special? And extra food since I won't get breakfast? And a treat before bedtime?" I wheedled.

Marianne laughed. "Yes, you can have something special AND a little extra AND a cookie before bed, if you really are hungry Wednesday night."

IF I'M HUNGRY? Oh dear Dog.

Chow for now!
Mars

PEERLESS PATRINA

My predecessor, Parker, was the fifth puppy Marianne and John raised for Canine Companions. Parker decided he did not want to be a working dog and is living with our friends Jeannie and Rod here in Denver. He's very happy living as a beloved pet along with their other lab, Nicky.

But his sister, oh, Parker's amazing sister, Peerless Patrina! She wanted to work, and is she ever doing a fabulous job! Patrina graduated as a Facility Dog and is working at ECLC of New Jersey, a school that provides special education for children five to twenty-one years of age. The school started a program in 2009 called "Learning is Unleashed," which won a state Innovations in Special Education award. Patrina is considered to be a full-time canine educator; she "helps students in a wide variety of ways in academic, motivational, and behavioral settings and physical, occupational, and speech therapy." Whew. I'm exhausted just typing that.

Cheryl is Patrina's partner. I asked her exactly what kinds of things she and Patrina do together. Here's what she told me:

"Every day at school is different; we never know what we may be doing. We might sit with a student who is working on academics, which helps the student focus. Patrina often reads with students, which fosters self-esteem since Patrina is non-judgmental. I make myself invisible during this time, so it's just the student reading to Patrina. Sometimes we are called to assist a specific student who needs motivation to accomplish a task or has had a meltdown and refuses to move. Patrina can ALWAYS get them focused, up, and moving again. There are particular students that work for 'Patrina time.' That time can include a walk, some quiet petting, or brushing her teeth or her coat. Our physical and occupational therapists look for new ideas using Patrina. She's even done partner yoga! She helps the students hold a pose, which is hard for our kids due to their lack of muscle control. The student assumes a pose and, if possible, Patrina goes underneath the student. This provides support and helps the student get a good stretch from the pose.

"It's been a real life changing event for me, to see how the kids respond to Patrina, and how she can get them to do things that teachers and therapists just can't. Incorporating Patrina into regular classroom lessons opens a whole new avenue to teach the same old thing. (How many cups of food are in Patrina's bag of dog food? How much does she weigh?)

"Our students are also learning about community service by making donations to Canine Companions. One of our classrooms put out a donation box, then took the money to the bank on a class trip to have the money counted and sent it to Canine Companions as a thank you for Patrina. Most importantly, having Patrina in our building has made ECLC a happier place. Even our staff is happier and smiles more easily when she is around!"

Chow for now!
Mars

NOW FOR SOME AMAZING CANINE COMPANIONS MAGIC...

You might remember that Patrina was raised by Dave and Regina, the same PRs raising my brother Madden. Several years ago, they attended a family gathering at a hotel. Along with them was Doug the Dog, their fifth Canine Companions puppy in training, who was then a gangly nine-month-old teenager. A young woman who worked at the hotel approached them, asking a million questions about Canine Companions and puppy raising. Dave and Regina obligingly gave her all the details and went on about their business.

Fast forward several years to Patrina's graduation.

When Dave and Regina met Patrina's partner at graduation, they asked how she became interested in Canine Companions. She replied that she'd been working a second, part-time job at a hotel several years earlier and met some puppy raisers, with a Golden Retriever puppy, who told her all about it. She was very interested in raising a puppy, but had had to put it off. When the time was finally right, she went to the director of ECLC, explained that she wanted to raise a Canine Companions pup, and asked if she could bring the pup to school during the day. The director suggested that she apply instead for a Facility Dog for the school, and she could be the facilitator.

The rest, as they say is history. I'm sure you've figured out that Patrina's partner, Cheryl, was the young woman at the hotel that day.

Wow.

Just. Wow.

Chow for now!
Mars

THE LIFE THAT WAS URIAH

Marianne's heart is heavy again. She received very sad news from her friend Jill about her Canine Companions Hearing Dog, Uriah, who passed away recently. Marianne let me read the tribute that Jill wrote about Uriah, and it was so beautiful and powerful that I just had to share it with you. THIS is what Canine Companions dogs are all about. I only hope that someday I can be as special to someone as Uriah was to Jill. What an honor that would be.

You will need a handkerchief to read this. Go get one now.

Dear Friends and Family,

It is with the saddest of hearts that I have to tell you that my beloved Hearing Dog, Uriah, passed away. He turned twelve in January, so I was blessed to have him in my life as long as I did. He was my sidekick, my best friend and my ears. We were as tight as two peas in a pod, perfectly matched and suited for each other. We traveled to Japan, England, Canada, Mexico, and all over the US to talk about assistance dogs. I felt safe and secure with my boy by my side and loved traveling with him, knowing that he would be my ears and help me hear the things I could not.

He collapsed ten years to the day from when I brought him home to Kansas to begin our hearing team partnership after graduating from Canine Companions for Independence. He was rushed to the emergency vet clinic, where I was told that the collapse was caused by fluid buildup around his heart. The ultrasound also revealed a tumor on his heart, the deadly cancer called hemangiosarcoma. My life as I knew it changed in that moment hearing the diagnosis. The vet gave him days, weeks, months; she really didn't know.

I always told him that it would be wonderful if we could be a hearing team for ten years, thinking to myself we would enjoy retirement together, but I never dreamed that he would take it literally. I should have known he would do as I asked; he always did. Until the end of his life, he did his best to alert me to what I could not hear. On his own, he modified his alerting, and I learned to pick up on those cues whenever he was letting me know that a sound was happening for me. He still wanted to do his job, and who was I to not let him do so? It made him happy, and he was as devoted to me as I was to him.

After his diagnosis he had more good days than bad, and I am very grateful for that. It was the hardest thing I ever had to do in my life to tell him that when it was his time to be free and let go, I would be okay. I told him that I loved him and I knew how much he loved me. I also told him that he only had to wait, he knew what that meant; I told him I would be back, he knew *what that meant too. The end was quick and I was there by his side. I didn't cry until his heart stopped beating, I didn't want him to think there was anything wrong.*

Now it will be the hardest thing in my life to move forward without my beloved boy by my side. I will be eternally grateful that Uriah picked me. We had a magnificent life together, and I am so very grateful for everyone who made it possible for Uriah to become a part of my life and their lives as well.

Thank you, Uriah, for everything. Thank you for the incredible journey we took together. You blessed my life every single day we had with each other. Thank you for all the love and joy you gave to me and brought into my life. You were an extraordinary Hearing Dog, a loving and devoted partner and a faithful friend to all. Rest in peace, my love, and don't forget: wait *and know that I will be back.*

With love and gratitude for the life that was Uriah,
Jill Exposito.

Please pass the tissues. Chow for now.
Mars

Boot Camp

It's difficult to decide whether growing pains are
something teenagers have — or are.
—Author Unknown

I'm a little over nine months old now and I seem to have become something called a "teenager."

Note to other Canine Companions puppies: You've reached adolescence when your puppy raiser says "NO!" and "DON'T!" more often than "Good dog." I notice that Marianne seems to be gritting her teeth a lot and correcting me for EVERY LITTLE THING.

Really, she is being ridiculously picky. For instance, I just wanted to sniff another dog when we were at Yogurt Guru last week. I admit I might have bolted without warning to the end of my leash, nearly causing Marianne to drop her dish of yogurt, but did she have to get nose-to-nose with me and lecture me, right there in the yogurt shop with all those cute girls watching? I was so embarrassed for her; I stared off into the middle distance and pretended I didn't know who she was.

A few days later we were going to tea and I got really excited when I saw my Auntie Jessica. I didn't realize Marianne was lollygagging behind me (humans walk so slowly!) and I … um … kind of yanked the leash a tiny bit. OK, I yanked the leash pretty good but I was still quite surprised when I heard the crash behind me and saw Marianne in a heap with the contents of her purse all around her. Sooo undignified. "White pants!" she moaned. "New sandals!" I dunno why she was so upset—it was just a skinned knee and a banged-up toe. The blood came out of the pants, and you really can't see the blood splotches on her sandals any more.

It really sends Marianne over the edge when I open the door to the closet where the litter box is kept and help myself to a snack. I've tried to explain that I'm a HELPER DOG and I'm helping her clean the litter box, but the third time she caught me in the closet in the same afternoon, she ordered me into my crate for my "own good." Harrumph. I was ready for a nap anyhow.

While I was in the crate napping Marianne called Vanessa.

"What's up?" I asked later when she let me out of the crate.

"You are going over to Vanessa and Kevin's for some boot camp with Chisum," and she laughed in a spooky way that gave me chills.

Uh-oh. I'd heard of The Legend of Chisum. See, Chiz was the first puppy Vanessa and Kevin raised. He was released from Canine Companions for a medical condition. Because they wanted to keep raising Canine Companions puppies, and because they had their keeper dog, Theo, they decided that Chisum should go live with the family that had his mom.

Chisum had other plans, however. He told animal communicator Terri O'Hara that he wasn't leaving. Vanessa explained that, while they adored him, they felt it would be best if he went to live with his mom. Chiz snorted and said "HA!" He told Terri he was going to say and help Vanessa and Kevin raise puppies. Vanessa and Kevin recognized the futility of their plans and agreed that Chisum should stay with them as the official Assistant Puppy Raiser.

Chisum is serious about his life's work, and he's been very, very successful. How successful, you ask? Vanessa and Kevin's second puppy, Phlox, graduated in November 2007. Their third puppy, Tommy, graduated in May 2009. Their fourth puppy, Dennie, is set to rotate through Team Training next month. If all goes well and he makes a match, Dennie will graduate in August.

That's a one hundred percent success rate for Chisum. True story. You have my paw of honor.

Word on the street is that Chiz doesn't take any nonsense from puppies, so when Marianne said I was going to Chizzy's Boot Camp I gulped. I had a feeling I was in for some tough love.

I spent almost a week with Chisum, and he was very strict with me. On walks I was not allowed to tug on the leash. He kept an eye on me in public and told me to behave. He reminded me to restrain myself when we saw other dogs. He made sure my *under* command was perfect. The list goes on and on! I was exhausted every night and was glad to collapse in the crate for R & R. I must admit, I learned lots, and Marianne seems happier with me. I'm home again and glad to have playtime with Meryl. But I am well aware that I'd better mind my manners, or it's back to boot camp!

Chow for now!
Mars

THE NAME GAME

"What is his name?" is the question Marianne hears most frequently, right after "Now, what kind of dog is he?"

My name is Mars, just plain Mars. Not Mars II or IV or XXX. I am the FIRST Mars. I find that very cool indeed.

When Marianne asked about my name, Marti Madias (my litter's breeder caretaker) said, "We thought, 'Mars: God of War, planet—how could he not be destined for great things?'" Yeah, what she said!

"So what?" you're thinking. "My dog is CoCoBug Bananapants the First. What's the big deal?"

Stay with me, here. Canine Companions' is a national breeding program, with puppy raisers in most every state, which translates into a lot of puppies—something like nine hundred every year!

Now, imagine naming that many puppies, keeping in mind that the dog will be a working dog in public. We try to be unobtrusive; "I didn't even see him!" is a huge compliment to a puppy raiser. CoCoBug Bananapants is not an unobtrusive dog name. Might work for a cat.

Anyhow, Canine Companions has a method for naming puppies. Each litter is assigned a letter, and all the pups in that litter have names beginning with that letter. They cycle through the alphabet numerous times each year, skipping some letters like Q, U, and X. I mean, who wants a puppy named Xylophone?

Some names are suggested by the breeder caretaker of the litter. Some names honor particular volunteers or donors. Marianne says that a popular auction item at fundraisers is the right to name a puppy. Why, she heard that Dean Koontz once bid $500,000 to name a puppy Gerda, after his lovely wife. He won, too. (We love Dean and Gerda Koontz for so many reasons.)

Canine Companions won't use a name that is currently in use until that dog is either released from the program, retires, or passes away. So I hope to be the one and only Mars for a l-o-n-g time. However, if there is ever another puppy named Mars, he'll be Mars II. Marianne's last pup was Ross VI, if you can imagine such a thing.

Some names leave the puppy raisers asking each other "Where did the Naming Fairy come up with that one?!?"

For example, there's a puppy coming to Colorado next month called GlenBell. Kind of odd, until you find out that the puppy is named for Glen Bell, the founder of Taco Bell (yum ... tacos ...), who was quite a philanthropist.

As for my littermates?

Miwa was named for a family friend who donated part of her liver to her very ill little sister about the time we were born. (Both are now doing great.) How could you not name a puppy after someone like that?!

Molina was named for Giants catcher Bengie Molina, and Madias is named for our super-fab breeder caretaker. Marco was named for several Marcos in the Madias family. Micron was just a fun, nerdy name. Madden was for Raiders coach John Madden, and Meryl and Marlena were suggestions from another breeder caretaker.

Personally, I can't think of a nicer honor than having a puppy named for you or someone you love. I guess that's why it's always a popular auction item, maybe not always half-a-million-dollars popular, but a hot item, nevertheless.

Chow for now!
Mars (the First)

GRADUATIONS

Yup, that's GRADUATIONS—PLURAL!

Well, every graduation includes more than one dog and one person, but what I mean is that FOUR, count 'em, FOUR Denver dogs are graduating this weekend.

Dennie is graduating as a Service Dog with a young man from Texas, whose brother also has a Canine Companions dog.

Holmby is graduating as a Service Dog with a young man from Texas too. (Not such a coincidence, I guess; from what I hear, Texas is a BIG state.)

Yori is graduating as a Facility Dog with a teacher from California who works with functionally non-verbal kids. Yori will help motivate the kids and perhaps even encourage them to speak in order to give him commands.

And last, but most exciting in this household, Ross is graduating as a breeder.

You can see why there might be some "Alleluias!" around here this week.

Many from the Denver Village are headed to Oceanside for graduation at the Southwest campus, but Marianne and John are headed to Santa Rosa, California, for Ross's official presentation as a breeder at the Northwest campus.

You may remember that we found out that Ross was selected as a breeder in February. In fact, he's had several "dates" already and there are two litters "on the ground" as they say. The F litter was sired by both Ross and Saris, with Dawna. Yeah, I know that's a little weird, but Canine Companions sometimes uses two breeder boys. Anyhow, those puppies went to puppy raisers last week! Their names are Feather, Fawn, Fluffy, Felipe, Funston, Fergenson, Finnian, Fitz, and Farina.

Ross also sired the H litter, and those puppies are going out to puppy raisers this week. We don't have a list of names other than

Hedwig and Hagrid. (The Naming Fairy must be a Harry Potter fan.) Marianne is hopeful that we might see an H puppy at graduation on Friday. Puppy breath!

Did I mention that I'm going along? Yes indeed, I will meet Ross (who left for professional training before I arrived in Denver) and his breeder caretakers, M-L (Mighty Lovely! *wink*) and Bill. I'm very excited, though Marianne has made it abundantly clear that I am to be on my Very Best Behavior. Or Else. I'm not exactly sure what "or else" means, but it doesn't sound like "extra cookies."

Well, I'd better start packing my suitcase (toy, food, cookies, clean-up bags, cookies, chewy bone, cookies) and practicing my commands.

Chow for now!
Mars

HOW DO YOU GIVE THEM UP?

Since I've been with Marianne and John I bet I've heard people ask them at least 2,642 times, "How will you be able to give Mars up?" As I get closer and closer to graduation, I am tempted to let Marianne begin the standard response: "With a big box of tissues in the morning …" and then finish it myself: " … and really big margaritas in the afternoon." That would give them a shock!

For all who still doubt you could turn in a puppy, I give you the following speech from Amy Thompson at this month's Northwest campus graduation. Amy's son Rob graduated with Skilled Companion Deirdre, and Amy was chosen as the class speaker. She was eloquent and funny and she made every single person in the audience cry. Even me. What, you think dogs don't cry? All I could think was, "Some day I want to be the subject of a speech like Amy's!"

Anyhow, read this and tell me how you could NOT give back a Canine Companions puppy? Even one as cute as I am. Oh, and you'd better have the tissues handy. Don't say I didn't warn you.

I'm so honored to speak on behalf of this summer's Skilled Companion Class. Our class is a diverse group of children and adults who came together to learn to work with a dog that would improve their lives. Each of you has inspired me with your strength and perseverance. Thank you all for your openness and support. It has been a gift to work with these people and share this experience with them. Each team has its own remarkable story. I'd like to share ours.

I first heard about Canine Companions for Independence three years ago, when a former student of mine reconnected with me. I still remember her as a smart, shy, seventh grader who was happy to be invisible in a group of people. She generously extended an invitation to visit her workplace and tour the facilities. It sounded like fun. She even sent me brochures and a calendar from her work with her picture on them. I kept the calendar posted in my classroom and told all my classes and fellow teachers about Shelley Dickinson, Canine Companions instructor.

A year after I heard from Shelley, our son, Rob, was in a car accident, and our lives changed dramatically. Days were filled with therapy sessions and medical procedures. I spent hours on the phone or filling out forms for services and equipment that Rob needed. We learned how to suction a tracheotomy tube, feed Rob through a tube in his stomach, use a lift to move him from a bed to a wheelchair, administer medications, all while we continued to hope that Rob would talk and walk again.

So, when a dear friend said, "You should contact your former student about getting a dog for Rob," I thought, "That's crazy. I don't have enough time in a day to keep up with the things I have to do, why would I add something else to my list of responsibilities?"

But what I said was, "That's a good idea." And I thought about it.

I thought about it during school vacations, when more and more of Rob's friends stopped coming home from college. I thought about it when Rob would call his cat to come and cuddle and the cat wouldn't come because Rob's hospital bed and air mattress spooked him. I thought about it a lot and knew it was indeed a good idea.

We finally came up to Canine Companions to visit after we got a wheelchair van for Rob. Shelley gave us a tour and a demonstration with a dog that wasn't ready for a recipient. As we watched her work the dog we couldn't figure out why this dog wasn't ready. He was clearly the best-trained dog we had ever seen. Shelley commanded sit and the dog sat. We didn't understand the dog should be sitting right next to the chair every time. Even after Shelley said, "See?" and corrected an imperfect "sit" position, we whispered to each other, "We'd take this dog in a heartbeat, he's amazing, he's perfect."

Even before we left Canine Companions that day, we knew we wanted a dog for Rob. So, like all the recipients, I started the application process and waited. I was thrilled when we got the call inviting us to this Team Training.

Then I got nervous.

Charles Schulz once said, "Try not to have a good time ... this is supposed to be educational." I'm certain he didn't say it about Canine Companions for Independence, because being with these people and these dogs is a good time. But, before I got here, I was ready for educational. I read and I highlighted and I studied the handouts, commands, and lectures that were sent to us. I knew, or thought I knew, how much went into preparing a dog for us. I wanted to be as prepared as possible. I didn't want Shelley to shake her head and say "See?"

I wasn't expecting the good time. By the end of the first day, the instructors relieved much of my anxiety. I began to believe I could be a pack leader AND it could be fun.

I knew the instructors were gifted professionals. That was obvious. They cared so much. They were so patient and

consistent. And that's just how they treated the dogs. But when Chuck fitted me for a prong collar because I wouldn't follow the sit *command, I knew they meant business.*
[laughter]

I also wasn't expecting the camaraderie in the dorm. Rob's been in a wheelchair for two years. To stay in a place that was so wheelchair-friendly, and on a beautiful campus, was a bonus. The adults in the dorm served as role models for all of us on how to live as independently as possible with grace and dignity; the lunches from the volunteers and the dedication of everyone connected with Canine Companions combined to support us.

But the dogs.

Honestly, how can anyone come to Canine Companions without falling in love with these dogs?

Of course they are adorable. That's a given. But I had no idea how smart they were. It wasn't until the third day here that I came to the realization that my goal was to try to learn everything the dogs already knew. We all came to Canine Companions to get a dog to help in our lives.

Since we've gotten our dogs there have been distinct images that I will carry with me: Patrick sitting outside Deckle's crate in the classroom; Tyler sitting on an armchair with Adonis in his lap; Stuart walking beside Ritzy in the mall; Jake snuggling on a blanket with Mindy; Deirdre and Rob asleep on Rob's bed. All magic moments that wouldn't be possible without Canine Companions.

Snoopy once said of Charlie Brown, "All his life he tried to be a good person. Many times, however, he failed, for after all, he was only human. He wasn't a dog."

We are only human, but how lucky we are to be paired with such exceptional dogs. Our puppy raiser is here today and we are lucky enough to get the first dog she has trained. Gratitude does not begin to cover the feelings we have for her and the other puppy raisers. People who take their time and money to raise, socialize, train, and then give these dogs up are nothing short of miracles.

> *This experience, having the dogs, brings families and people together in a way nothing else does. More than a good time, more than educational, this experience has been amazing. Every dog, every staff member, and every person we have met and worked with these past two weeks has touched us. It's fitting that we attended Team Training at the Jean and Charles Schulz Canine Companions Campus because, as Charles Schulz said, "Happiness is a warm puppy."*

sigh

Chow for now!
Mars

PHOTO SHOOT

A few days ago I found Marianne rummaging around in the closet.

I stood and watched her for a minute. "What are you looking for?" I asked.

Marianne jumped and looked guilty. "Nothing much. You'll see later," she replied evasively. "Hey, I have good news! Alexa is coming over this afternoon." She patted my head and walked away with the box.

This seemed like a suspiciously abrupt change of subject, but I didn't press for details. I went to tell Meryl and Mina that Alexa was coming over and Marianne was acting funny.

"Uh-oh," said Mina. "Was she looking through the box in the closet?"

"Yeah, she was," I said. "Why?"

Meryl shivered. Mina shook her head. "You were too little to remember much about Christmas last year, but that box has the holiday costumes in it. She's probably going to make us wear funny hats and collars."

Meryl sighed and said, "And Alexa is her photographer friend?" Mina nodded.

"Uh-oh is right," I thought.

Sure enough, when Alexa arrived she had her camera. We went into the backyard and Marianne followed with the box from the closet. I heard jingling and before I knew what was happening I was wearing a velvet collar with bells on it. Meryl and Mina looked resigned and let Marianne put jingle bell collars around their necks, too.

"Don't fight it," advised Meryl. "It's no use."

Alexa had us pose in different places in the yard. She's a kind and talented photographer and lets us be ourselves—as much as we can with costumes on. Meryl and I got a little silly and played chase with one of the hats and tug-of-war with the antlers. But Alexa was patient and let us run around in between posed shots.

Afterwards, Marianne looked through the photos and chose some of them for a holiday card to send out to friends and family. I guess the costumes were worth the hassle since I think we look pretty cute. And since Marianne takes terrible pictures (blurry, thumb in the way, heads cut off), at least she'll have these to remember me by.

Chow for now!
Mars

BARK LESS, WAG MORE

I wandered into the study where Marianne was sitting at the desk. She was deep in concentration as I peered at the computer screen. She seemed to be making a long list of some kind.

"What's that?" I asked. "It looks like the world's longest to-do list."

Marianne laughed. "It IS the world's longest to-do list. These are things I plan to do in 2011."

"Oh no, not New Year's resolutions! I hate New Year's resolutions," I whined. "I remember last year and how awful it was and how hard it was and how you made me agree to dozens of resolutions and ..."

"Oh, stop," Marianne interrupted. "You remember nothing of the kind. You were three and a half months old and the only resolution I suggested for you was to remember to *hurry* outside instead of inside." She frowned at me. "Why are you so wound up?"

I shrugged sheepishly. "Well, I guess I'm worried about what's to come in 2011. I'm in the advanced puppy class now and going to professional training in May. That's a lot of pressure!"

Marianne sat down on the floor and pulled me into her lap. "Oh, Mars, I didn't know you were so worried about things. I'm sorry if I'm pressuring you to do well." She rubbed my tummy. "You are a good boy and I know you'll do your best in class this spring. And when you go to professional training in May the trainers will help you to learn new commands. You have so much potential, I just want you to be the best you can be."

I held up my front paws for a massage. "I know you weren't happy with some of the things on the puppy-sitter report you saw this morning. I guess I could have been better behaved, huh?" I sighed. I'd had a wonderful time spending the week with another puppy raiser family and my classmate Hendrix while Marianne and John were on vacation, but I didn't realize that Donna was paying attention and taking notes!

Marianne nodded. "Just because we were on vacation doesn't mean you were on vacation. Your sitter report was terrible." She stopped rubbing my paws and frowned at me again. "Let's review the naughtiness, shall we? Jumping on the bed, snacking on the plants in the living room, barking when you were in your crate, and SLEEPING ON THE COFFEE TABLE." She shook her head. "Mars, that is NOT a good report."

Yikes. When she listed everything out like that, it was worse than I thought.

"It wasn't all bad, was it?" I asked meekly.

"You were given good marks for behaving in public and for greeting people appropriately," Marianne said. "I am very happy about those things, but we are going to work on those other behaviors in 2011. In fact," she said, standing up, "we are going to start right now. *Kennel!*"

"Now? In the middle of the day?" I gasped. "But ..."

"Nu-uh, Buster. *Kennel!*" and she pointed to the bedroom.

Uh-oh. When she calls me "Buster" it's all over. I slunk into the crate and grumbled when she locked the door. I barked a few times in protest.

"Stop that! You have your stuffed bear and a chewie, so just settle down. I'll let you out in a while and we'll work on *down-stays*," Marianne said.

Oh, joy. I guess I know what my New Year's resolutions are going to be. As the saying goes: Wag more, bark less. Sit. Stay.

Chow for now!
Mars

HIPPITY HOP

Our small kitty had a mishap this week. Dewey likes to sleep on the top of the tall bookcase in the living room and when he jumps down he usually lands on the easy chair before he hits the floor. But on Tuesday night he skipped the chair and landed directly on the floor with a THUD. I ran over to see if he was OK.

Dewey said "**@!*!" and stalked away, limping.

Later we heard Mina making her anxious, squeaky "Timmy's in the well!" noise, so John went to see what was wrong. He found Mina in the hallway, squeaking and pointing at Dewey who was huddled in the coat closet.

"I think Dewey hurt himself," John said, carrying Dewey into the living room. He gently set Dewey down, and we watched as he limped across the room.

"**@!*!," Dewey said. "OUCH!!"

"I guess we're going to see the vet tomorrow," Marianne told him. Dewey groaned.

Marianne patted him. "Sorry, puss, but we have to get your paw checked."

Dewey crawled under the rocking chair and glowered at her. I was worried; Dewey is always happy and purring. He's never grumpy.

The next day Marianne shut me in my crate before she took Dewey to the vet. "I want to come!" I protested. "Dewey needs me!" I whined.

Marianne shook her head. "Not this time, Mars. You can comfort him when we get home." I sulked. Is this any way to treat a helper dog?

I woke from my nap when they returned, and Marianne unlatched my crate. Meryl, Mina, and I raced into the living room to see Dewey. I gaped in shock when Marianne unzipped the travel crate. Dewey flung himself out and hobbled unsteadily into the kitchen. Mina and Meryl followed, sniffing him anxiously.

"What is that huge thing on his leg?" I asked. "It's bigger than he is!"

"It's a splint to help his leg heal," Marianne said. "It's big so that he can't put his weight on it and put more stress on his leg."

We walked into the kitchen and watched Dewey hop-stomp across the floor. He looked like a very grouchy pirate.

"He doesn't look happy," I said. "Dewey, are you OK?"

Dewey stopped and snorted. "Do I look OK?" he snarled. "!#@@@!!*!!" I blushed; that's not a word I'm allowed to use.

Marianne sighed. "Oh, boy, this is going to be interesting. I guess we'll have to lift you onto the counter for meals," she told Dewey.

Meryl, Mina, and I swiveled our heads in unison toward her. "MEALS?"

Marianne laughed. "Yes, OK, it's a little early, but I'll fix your dinner now." We drooled in anticipation as Marianne measured out our kibble. Food, glorious food!

After she set our bowls down, she fixed Dewey's food and lifted him onto the counter. As I was licking up the last of my kibble I was startled by a crash. Dewey's dish was on the floor.

"What happened?" I asked. Marianne looked puzzled. "I don't know," she said, picking up the dish.

Meryl cleaned up the cat food on the floor while Marianne fixed another dish for Dewey. Dewey bent to eat, flinging his splint sideways, sending the dish skittering across the counter. Marianne caught it before it hit the floor and said, "I guess we'll have to rig an elevated dish." She found a box and set the dish on it, holding it in place as Dewey scarfed down the rest of his dinner.

"I'll figure out something better," she promised as she carefully lifted Dewey to the floor. He hop-stomped around the kitchen, shaking his paw in frustration. Meryl warily backed away.

"I look ridiculous in this thing," Dewey snarled. "And how am I supposed to jump to the top of the bookcase for my nap?"

"NO JUMPING!" Marianne exclaimed in horror. "You'll have to nap in a bed on the floor. I'll fix it so it's nice and warm, I promise." Dewey watched dubiously as Marianne arranged a kitty bed and blanket in the den.

Later, I was dozing and Marianne was watching the news when we heard a series of thumps and crashes from the kitchen. We ran out and Marianne flipped on the light. Dewey was standing on top of the refrigerator.

"How on earth did you do that?" she gasped, staring at Dewey, who looked quite pleased with himself.

He grinned. "I've figured out how to get around with this silly splint," he said. "It just takes a little more effort is all."

Marianne carefully reached up and lifted him down to the counter. "PLEASE be careful," she begged. "I'd rather you didn't jump right now. How about if I put a chair by the counter so you can get up with less effort and skip the jump to the frig?"

Dewey shrugged. "Up to you, but it's really not necessary. Watch!" And he hop-stomped across the counter, flinging his paw sideways and scattering silverware, plates and a salt shaker in his wake. Marianne grabbed for things before they fell off the counter.

"Dewey, please stop!" She lifted him to the floor.

Dewey shook his head. "No, I'm getting really good at this," he said and hop-stomped rapidly out of the kitchen, smacking toys and dog dishes with his splint as he went.

Marianne muttered something under her breath

There was a thump and crash from the living room. Marianne hurried away to investigate.

Chow for now!
Mars

Sunday Funnies

We had a bit of excitement here on Sunday morning. Marianne and John were drinking coffee and reading the paper. I was lying on my back enjoying a sunbath, when suddenly Mina began barking hysterically and flinging herself at the back door.

"Intruder! Interloper! Fiend! Kill! Kill! Let me out so I can get it!"

Meryl jumped up and down by the door. "Out out out out out!!!!" Meryl's bark rattles the windows.

"Meryl, inside voice!" Marianne pleaded as she walked to the door.

I didn't see what was so exciting but I barked too. What the heck.

Marianne shoved us out of the way and peered outside. "What are you barking at? I don't see anything." She started to open the door to go out but Mina and Meryl shoved past her and galloped to the far corner of the backyard.

"GIRLS!" Marianne shouted, running after them. "Get back here!" I jogged along to see what was so interesting.

Meryl and Mina were barking furiously at something climbing on the telephone pole. It was too big to be a squirrel and didn't look like a cat, though it was about Dozer's size.

"Oh, I'm sorry!" Marianne said to the furry gray animal while trying to grab Meryl and Mina. "I really didn't mean to let them outside, but I promise they won't hurt you."

The creature climbed a little higher and glared at all of us. "Bah!" he spat.

"What is he?" I asked. "He has a funny face."

"Who you calling funny, curly boy?" he snarled at me. "Look who's talking about funny looking."

"It's a raccoon," Marianne explained, while Mina continued hurling curses at him.

And then, to our surprise, Meryl jumped over the fence into the yard behind ours. Whoa!

"MERYL!" gasped Marianne. "Get back here!"

Meryl stopped barking and jumping. She looked around in surprise. "How did I get here?"

Marianne looked up at the raccoon. "Sorry, buddy, you're on your own. I'd make a break for it if I were you." He looked around, shrugged, then hopped into the other neighbor's yard and vanished.

Marianne gestured frantically at Meryl. "Jump back over the fence right now! RIGHT NOW!"

Meryl shook her head. "No, I don't know how to jump over things. I'm not a jumper. Sorry."

This is true. Meryl won't jump over baby gates or laundry baskets. She won't even step over Dozer if he's blocking the hallway. She'll just stand in place and moan until Marianne tells Dozer to stop teasing her; whereupon, he saunters off, pleased with himself.

Marianne looked worried. The yard behind us isn't completely fenced and I knew she was concerned that Meryl would decide to go explore. She climbed over the fence and used her bathrobe sash to fashion a leash of sorts for Meryl. "I really don't want to walk you home," she told Meryl. "I'm in my jammies and slippers and not dressed for a walk through the neighborhood."

Meryl perked up. "Walk? I love that word, walk!"

"What should I do?" I asked.

"It would be helpful if you'd go get John," Marianne said.

Mina and I ran to the back door and barked, but nothing happened. Mina took off, sniffing the ground where the raccoon had been. I ran back to the fence, where Marianne was giving Meryl a pep talk.

"Look, it's not very high, only four feet. Just jump!" She lifted Meryl's front feet off the ground. "Please try."

Meryl wriggled away, panicked. "Too high!" she insisted. "I can't jump, it's way too high and scary."

Marianne sighed. She took the bathrobe sash-leash and carefully tied Meryl to the fence. "Stay right there!" she told Meryl and climbed back into our yard. She ran to the back door, flung it open, screamed "HELP!" and slammed it shut. She ran back to the fence where Meryl was nervously prancing around. "I don't want to be here. I want to go back inside and have a snack and a nap. Do something!"

John appeared, and Marianne filled him in. He looked at Meryl.

"Come on Meryl, jump!" he said. Marianne and I rolled our eyes. Yeah, right.

"You are going to have to go over there and lift her over the fence," Marianne told him. John sighed and climbed over the fence. He picked up Meryl.

"HELP!" Meryl yelped. "Why are you doing this? You're not Kevin!" She wiggled frantically. "Mars, go get Kevin!"

(Kevin is our puppy raiser friend and he picks up all dogs, regardless of size, even Meryl, who goes limp with delight. We love it when Kevin picks us up.)

Mina barked in alarm, I anxiously jumped up and down, and John staggered in circles toward the fence, juggling Meryl.

"Mars, stop it! Mina, hush!" Marianne scolded. "You're not helping!"

We backed away as Meryl launched herself away from John and over the fence. "HURRAY!" we shouted. Meryl looked relieved.

I heard something that sounded suspiciously like a raccoon snickering as we headed back into the house.

Chow for now!
Mars

WOMBAT

[Cue ominous, shark-approaching music from *Jaws* ...]

Dinah.

Remember that name. I predict you're going to see it in connection with a news story involving severed fingers or ears or tails.

Cunning creature that she is, she looks like a sweet little black Canine Companions puppy.

HA, I say. HA.

She is not a thirteen-week old puppy. Oh, no, my friends. She is a shark. With many, many sharp teeth and a lust for yelping victims. She is worse than all the other puppies put together. She has us all on the run. The only peace we have is when Marianne or John realizes Dinah has Meryl or Mina or me pinned mercilessly in her snapping jaws and declares the game over on account of Wombat. Dinah is then escorted into her crate or x-pen for a nap, and we retire to safe places to lick our wounds and recover.

"Wombat" is the code word around here for shark attack. I don't know why Marianne and John don't call it what it is, but apparently Wombat has been in use since the days of Stryker No, Stryker Don't, the second Canine Companions puppy they raised.

"Why, oh why is she here?" I wailed. "Who asked for another puppy?"

Marianne sighed. "Here's the deal. Dinah was with another puppy raiser whose circumstances changed and she couldn't keep Dinah. We offered to foster her for a little while."

"Huh," I snorted. "Easy for you to be generous. It's not your ears she thinks are tug toys."

Meryl flapped an ear at me. "I remember when you were that age, and I have the scars to prove it."

I was insulted. "I was never that bad," I said. "No one ever called me `Wombat.'"

Meryl and Mina fell against each other howling. "Hoo, boy, how quickly they forget," Mina giggled helplessly. Meryl nodded and pointed at me. "Wombat," she said. She and Mina cracked up again.

Annoyed, I turned and stalked away. Really, I was NEVER like that. Yes, I had sharp teeth. Yes, I had to be reminded to play nicely. But I was not a Wombat!

I went to find Marianne in the kitchen, where she was loading the dishwasher. "So how long is she here for?" I asked.

"A couple months is all. And here's some good news for you: we are co-fostering her with Vanessa and Kevin, so some of the time she will be at their house."

"Wow, that is excellent news!" I said. "Who is going to raise her after that?"

Marianne shut the dishwasher door. "More really good news; Diane and Elizabeth can take her when she's a little older."

"Have you mentioned this to Calhoun?" I asked. Calhoun is Diane and Elizabeth's current Canine Companions puppy and my friend. I have to look out for his ears, too.

Marianne shook her head. "No, but about the time they take her Calhoun will be off to professional training with you."

I glanced over at Dinah, who was sound asleep in the crate, all four feet in the air, snoring loudly.

"She is kind of cute," I admitted. "When she and all of her teeth are asleep, anyhow."

Meryl whispered to Mina, "Shall we tell him about Puppy #8 arriving in April or May?"

"Nah," Mina said. "Let him live in ignorance a little longer."

Chow for now!
Mars

DAZZLING DEIRDRE

Remember how I went to graduation in August at our Northwest campus in Santa Rosa and then blogged about the wonderful graduation speech by Amy Thompson? Her son Rob was partnered with Skilled Companion Deirdre.

Periodically, Marianne checks Rob's Caring Bridge journal for Amy's updates. She was reading some of the updates yesterday, and I heard a sniffle. I peered out at her from my bed under the desk.

"Are you OK?" I asked, concerned.

Marianne nodded sheepishly. "Yes, sometimes these updates are so cool that I get all choked up."

"Really? Like what?"

"Like this one," Marianne said, reading Amy's journal update aloud:

> This morning, Rob was in the computer room and I was doing some laundry, a typical Saturday morning. As I walked back into the room, Rob's right hand was stretched out and he was petting Deirdre while she stood on the mat table next to Rob's chair.
>
> I realized that Deirdre deserves the credit for Rob's improved moods and motivation. In the six months since she's been here, she and Rob have really bonded. I rarely need to tell her to wait with Rob. She's already there. When Rob's in his wheelchair and starts to move, she's up and following him before we even think to give a command.
>
> When Deirdre is out in public with us, often people will ask, "What does she do for Rob?"
>
> My usual answer is, "She takes his socks off at night and puts them in the laundry basket." I'm not sure exactly how to describe what she does for Rob. She helps him sleep. She helps him stretch his hand and arm out. She keeps him company. She loves him.

I nodded my head. "That is very cool, but not really a Kleenex Moment, as you puppy raisers say."

"You are one tough puppy," Marianne told me. "This entry should do it."

> There was a group of kids on a field trip at Canine Companions today. They seemed to be having fun, as kids always do during a field trip. I wish they could understand what a magic place it is. How the work they do really does change people's lives in such a positive way.
>
> As I type, Rob and Deirdre are in the bed next to mine. Rob is talking in his sleep and Deirdre is snuggled up to his side. Adorable. Comforting. Reassuring. They make a good team.

"Yes," I gulped. "That one is Kleenex-worthy. Anything else?"

"This one just made me smile," Marianne said, as she began to read again:

> One of the parts of the test [at the mall] is to drop the leash and keep walking. One instructor stands where they want you to drop the leash, and another stands where you can pick it up. After doing this during Team Training in August and practicing, it seems pretty routine. All the dogs just keep walking next to their handler. I suppose it's part of the test to make sure the dog is still under control and doesn't run off.
>
> As Rick dropped the leash, Deirdre paused, looked at Rick, who continued to walk as directed. Then she looked at the leash, reached down and picked it up and trotted it up to Rick. Classic Canine Companions dog, making the handler look great.

We looked at each other. "Wow," said Marianne. "Do you think you could be that good someday?"

"Pfff," I snorted. "I'm that good now!" I picked up my leash and wagged my tail. "I make you look good every day!'

"Yes, you do," she agreed. "Now let's see if you can do that with the trainers when you go to professional training in May."

Chow for now!
Mars

RAMBAM'S LADDER

I watched Marianne pull a sheet of paper off the printer and tape it to our office door.

I squinted. "What is that?"

"It's a flyer advertising an informational meeting in a few weeks for folks who are interested in becoming Canine Companions puppy raisers," she replied. "You went to one last spring, remember?"

"No, not really," I admitted. "Was I awake for it?"

Marianne laughed. "Well, you were only about six months old, so yes, you probably slept through all but the part at the end where people petted you."

I yawned. "That's the best part anyhow." I walked closer to the door and stared at the flyer thoughtfully. "I've put it on my Facebook page," Marianne said. "We'll put up the flyers in other places, too."

"That flyer's a good start, but we need something to really grab people's attention," I said. "Ooh, I know! What was that bit that Food Lady wrote about somebody's ladder?"

"'Food Lady?' Oh, you mean Donna Black-Sword, your brother Micron's puppy raiser." She sat down at her desk and began typing. "I think I know what you're talking about. It's called 'Rambam's Ladder' and it was on her blog, *Puppy Raising by the Sword*. Here it is."

I climbed into her lap to get a better view of the screen. "Yeah, that's it!" I read a few lines. "Now that's how you get new puppy raisers! Grab their hearts and squeeze." I nodded in satisfaction. "I wonder if Food Lady would let me reprint this?"

"Her name is Donna, not Food Lady," Marianne said. "You could ask her."

"That's what Micron calls her," I said defensively. "Just like I call you ..." I stopped.

"Yes?" Marianne said dangerously.

"Nevermind," I replied hastily. "I'll just send Donna a note and ask if I can steal ... er ... borrow her blog."

Ever gracious, Donna said I could. Below is a portion of that post. I hope you like it as much as I do.

Rambam's Ladder

Not long ago, a coworker asked me: "If you were in a crowded room and someone yelled 'GEEK!' would you turn around?" Oh, ha ha, Funny Guy. Well, yeah, maybe. But only because I totally own it.

There's nothing wrong with having geek tendencies, you know. Ok, I will admit there may be a couple of drawbacks. My dog handling abilities somewhat overshadow my people skills, 'tis true. And I've never been a slave to fashion. That's sadly obvious to the general public as well.

But I can do amazing things with Photoshop and that's a skill that I wouldn't trade for any amount of cute shoes. And that fancy computer you're using to read this? I could take the thing down to individual parts and put it back together again, I could.

I'm certainly no expert in the ways of dog behavior, in spite of my inability to successfully interact with people. I'm only good with dogs because I love being around them. Let me brief you on the skills you need to be a volunteer puppy raiser. Do you love people and dogs? Wanna do something fun that will help bring someone independence? Well, there's a good start. Canine Companions isn't looking for professional dog handlers to raise these dogs. Instead, if you can offer a safe, consistent environment for these fuzzies and are willing to learn some basic training skills ... and you have a big heart, that'll about do it.

I know there are a lot of dog lovers out there. Micron and I meet you all the time during our outings. We hear your stories of the funny dogs you have, the beloved dogs you've lost. So, what are y'all doing for the next year and a half?

Oh, and that part about giving them up? No messing around with that. It is a hard thing to do. But you know what? It can be done. There are 1,082 of us doing it all the time. Some of us turn to a box of tissues and good friends at turn-in time.

Others take that box of tissues and set them right next to our margaritas. I'll leave you to wonder which I am.

I'm living a blessed life and want to give back in some way. I may be about the age of fellow geekster Bill Gates, but nowhere near his net worth. Philanthropy is not going to be my thing. Puppy raising for Canine Companions is fun and exciting and, best of all, something I can do. In my own small way, I can actually be part of something that will change someone's life. How cool is that? Pretty darn cool, I say.

In a prior life as a catechist, I taught a faith formation class for seventh grade kids. One of my favorite lesson plans for the Christmas season involved Julie Salamon's book Rambam's Ladder: A Meditation on Generosity and Why It Is Necessary to Give. Ms. Salamon tells us about Rabbi Moses ben Maimon, a twelfth century physician, philosopher, and scholar, also known by his Greek name, Maimonides, or by an acronym of his full name: RaMBaM. I'll be referring to him here as Rambam, as that's the title of the book, and because it's fun to say out loud.

Being knee-deep in the knowledge that seventh grade catechism students are newly self-aware, and just realizing there's a whole world in which to get into trouble, I appreciated any opportunity to discuss ways they could make the world a better place. My weapon of choice was Rambam's Ladder of Charity. Now, I won't hold you for an hour in a classroom while you sit on a cold, hard plastic chair and get told repeatedly to keep your hands to yourself. We're all grown-ups here, so let's just hit the highlights.

Rambam describes eight steps on the ladder, the bottom rung being "Reluctance: to give begrudgingly." That's when you give only because you feel you have to. It's a good thing, to be sure. But you can do better, he says.

You can give cheerfully, but less than is proper. Or donate only after being asked. Next up is giving before being asked, but risk making the recipient feel shame. Moving higher is to give to someone you don't know, yet ensuring that your name *is known as the donor. Even better, though, says Rambam, is to give to someone you know, but you remain anonymous.*

We've made it almost to the top: to give to someone you don't know and to do so anonymously.

So what's the top rung? What's the best we can do on this Ladder of Charity? That would be the Gift of Self-Reliance. Julie Salamon describes this as a gift or a loan, or to find work for the recipient, so that they never have to ask for help again. She gives examples of helping someone find gainful employment or start a business, as well as helping someone through an addiction.

This is pretty powerful stuff, and just a bit challenging to cram into a twelve-year-old's brain. But stuff it in there I did.

So, anyone seeing the connection to the work of Canine Companions for Independence? I do. I'm seeing a non-profit organization that enhances the lives of people with disabilities by providing trained assistance dogs and ongoing support to ensure quality partnerships. An organization that provides a new level of independence, free of charge.

This twelfth-century scholar certainly wasn't thinking about assistance dogs, of course. But I'm feeling the spirit of his intention is covered here. Hey, I'm no saint; ask my mom. Just kidding, don't ask my mom, please. (Hi Mom, I love you!). But I'm feeling good about what I'm trying to do with this puppy raising business. As all Canine Companions puppy raisers should.

You know, you could feel good about this too. Think about it. Pray on it. Then call Canine Companions and ask some questions about what it takes to be a puppy raiser. You'll love it, I promise you.

sigh Got you right in the heart, didn't she? Uh-huh.

Chow for now!
Mars

THE TURN-IN ZONE

Early mornings at Chez McKiernan can be kind of noisy and busy. This morning, Dozer, Dewey, Meryl, Mina, and I were all milling around, hoping for breakfast.

"Move," Marianne snarled as she tried to maneuver through kitchen. "You're all in my way." She smacked food dishes onto the counter and rattled kibble into them with unusual force.

"Uh-oh," said Meryl.

"Oooh, not good, not good at all," said Dewey, jumping to the relative safety of the counter.

Dozer hustled out of the kitchen. "I'll just wait here for my breakfast," he called from the Big Giant Closet. "No hurry."

Mina turned to me. "Run," she advised. "Hide."

"Before I eat?" I asked, incredulously. "No way."

"Your choice," Mina said. "I'll eat later." She trotted back to the bedroom.

Marianne handed out our dishes, poured a big mug of coffee, snarled at Dozer, who was blocking the doorway and left the room. I frowned. Marianne isn't a morning person, but this seemed extreme.

Meryl finished her breakfast, shambled over, and sat down. Mina poked her head around the door. "Is she gone? Is it safe to come in?" she whispered.

"Yes, she's gone," Meryl said. Turning to me, she asked, "When do you go to professional training?"

"I think we leave tomorrow," I answered. "Why?"

"That explains it," said Meryl.

"Yep, I thought so," agreed Mina.

"WHAT?" I demanded. "What does Marianne's mood have to do with me going to professional training?"

"Everything!" Meryl exclaimed.

"It's the Turn-in Zone," explained Mina. "I've been through this seven times now, and it's like this every time."

"The Turn-in Zone? What's that?" I wondered.

"A long, long, long time ago, there was a television show called *The Twilight Zone*," said Mina. "Each episode started with

> *There is a fifth dimension beyond that which is known to man. It is a dimension as vast as space and timeless as infinity. It is the middle ground between light and shadow, between science and superstition, and it lies between the pit of man's fears and the summit of his knowledge. This is the dimension of imagination. It is an area we call the Twilight Zone.*

I shivered. "That's spooky."

Mina went on. "Marianne and Vanessa decided that for puppy raisers this fifth dimension is called *The Turn-in Zone*. It goes like this:

> *There is a fifth dimension beyond that which is known to puppy raiser and puppy. It is a dimension as vast as space and timeless as infinity. It is the middle ground between tears and laughter, between awareness and denial, and it lies between the puppy raiser's hope for graduation and fear of release. This is the dimension of fuzzy thinking. It is an area we call the Turn-in Zone.*

"That's pretty funny!" I said.

"You'd think so, wouldn't you?" said Meryl. "But it's no laughing matter. The Turn-in Zone is real. For the next few days, Marianne is going to be grouchy, weepy, happy, sad, forgetful, and spacey. Be patient with her."

I still wasn't sure why Marianne was feeling so emotional. After all, she's known about this since the day I arrived. It's not as though turn-in is a big surprise. I decided to call my Auntie Dr. Elizabeth. She's a psychologist and a puppy raiser. I was sure she could help me figure it out.

After I explained my confusion, Auntie Dr. E said, "I'll try to answer in a way that makes sense to dogs, although it's going to be tough, because dogs are so good at living in the moment that it may be hard to picture what it's like in the human brain."

"The human brain is a complete mystery to me," I admitted. "You humans fret about so many things at the same time."

"We humans spend a lot of time living in different moments," agreed Auntie Dr. E. "You know how when you're getting a belly rub from Marianne that's all you're doing? You're just experiencing how good it feels to be right there with her right then. For a lot of us humans, if we're with someone we love, we may be thinking about how nice it is to be with them. And what it would be like if we couldn't be with them again. And when we might be with them again. And what we have to do between now and then. And how we're going to get the laundry done. And … You get the point."

"Yes, I think so," I said. "But what does that have to do with how Marianne is feeling this week?"

"So, our human brains are kind of like a four-lane highway, with lots of cars zipping along in and out of the lanes. Most of the time, there's enough space for all the traffic to move along pretty well. But when we have something big we're thinking about, especially if it's something that takes up a lot of space in our minds and our hearts, that something big can fill up three lanes on its own. That only leaves one lane for everything else—including where we put our cell phones or our car keys, or when to feed the dog. Things get jammed up in that other lane."

I was beginning to understand. "Go on."

"And that, Mars, is what we call the Turn-in Zone. We know from the day we get you—even before!—that we'll kiss you farewell and send you off to find your bliss. But when that day is very close, we turn it over and over in our minds until sometimes we feel like it's all we can see. Silly humans, sometimes we're so busy thinking about the time we WON'T have you, that we think about it when we DO have you! We could learn a lesson from you and your friends. I suspect that if we could learn to just be where we are we'd spend less time in the fuzzy thinking of the Turn-in Zone."

I pondered this. "You're turning in Calhoun on Saturday with me, aren't you? So are you in the Turn-in Zone this week, or are you living in the moment?"

There was a pause and I heard sniffling. "Turn-in Zone," said Auntie Dr. E in an oddly strained voice. "Darn it, Mars!" she squeaked and abruptly hung up.

"Ah," I said to myself. "Even the wise and learned puppy raisers can't avoid the Turn-in Zone."

Dr. Seuss once said: "Don't cry because it's over. Smile because it happened." Good advice, that; he was probably a dog in another life. But I have a feeling the puppy raisers will be sharing king—sized boxes of tissues and fishbowl-sized margaritas this coming Saturday after turn-in.

Chow for now!
Mars

EPILOGUE

Mars was released a mere three weeks after turn-in for kennel stress. Even though he had two canine roommates, Mars simply could not bear to be without human companionship at night, nor could he stand being crated in the training room during the day when the trainers worked with other dogs. Basically, Mars was released for being Mars: a Velcro love sponge.

We asked Canine Companions to place Mars in Thousand Oaks, California, with friends Judi and Greg, whose daughter Amy has a Canine Companions Facility Dog. Judi works from home most days, so Mars has *nearly* all the human companionship he desires. They also have three horses and a cat named Monster, all of whom have become Mars' fast friends. They have a swimming pool, and we're told Mars has made substantial improvements in his technique. He has even learned to throw his own tennis balls into the pool for retrieval. Greg surfs in his free time, so we fully expect to hear that he's taught Mars how to hang ten—er, eighteen—before the year is out.

Our eighth puppy, Rocket, is a goofy, happy puppy with a table-clearing Labby tail that never stops wagging. He brings us joy on a daily basis, except when we're cleaning up rolls of shredded toilet paper, admonishing him not to dig holes in the yard, and reminding him that the cat is not a toy. We have high hopes for him when he goes to professional training in November 2012.

And the beat goes on ...

ACKNOWLEDGMENTS

I owe thank yous to so many people for this book:

To Katherine Sears of Booktrope, who was an early fan of the DogBlogs and approached me about turning them into a book. I don't know how or if I would have taken the first step without her enthusiastic encouragement.

To the Powers That Be at KMGH-TV for not laughing me out of the newsroom when I first suggested the DogBlog as a feature of thedenverchannel.com, and for letting it continue lo these many years later.

To Jane Slade for her amazing, mad editing skills. Even though Jane was unfamiliar with Canine Companions for Independence, service dogs, and puppy raising, she understood the essence and meaning of Canine Companions right away. I knew we were a "perfect match" (Canine Companions humor) when she sent me an Excel spreadsheet, color coded to indicate which chapters to cut, which to keep, and which to revise, with detailed notes and thoughtful suggestions. This book is easily twice as good as it would have been without Jane's insightful, judicious, and sometimes humorous editing skills.

To my brother-out-law Ronald J. Allen, who has published so many books, he's modestly lost count (over 30—I checked), who kept telling me that I should write a book. Thank you for making me believe it was possible.

To Penny Blankenship for agreeing to illustrate this book on the strength of an email from me—a perfect stranger—because she likes dogs. Her drawings make me smile and/or giggle helplessly and are the icing on this particular cake. Not to mention, she made critical changes on deadline *while she was without power during Hurricane Sandy*! Penny rocks.

To fellow puppy raiser and author Jessica Swaim, for encouraging a fledgling writer over many cups of tea, from the very first DogBlog to the present. Cheers!

To all of my Canine Companions friends, dogs-in-law, and fellow puppy raisers, for reading the DogBlogs, suggesting topics, letting my puppies interview you and/or borrow your work, but most especially for sharing the journey.

And last, but most certainly not least, to the Denver Village (John McKiernan, Diane Brookshire, Elizabeth Holman, Chris and Jennifer Halstead, Vanessa Graziano, Kevin O'Grady, Pat Bird, Randi Price, Carol-Ann Goheen, Amber Urban), for being my friends, support network, fellow puppy raisers, and family. Here's to Friday Follies, turn-ins, and graduations for many years to come! Please pass the tissues and another margarita.

Made in the USA
Lexington, KY
11 February 2013